4 Stories Book

Hello readers,

A warm and heartfelt welcome to each one of you! Your presence here is the spark that ignites the magic of storytelling and transforms these words into a shared experience. Whether you're here for a momentary escape, seeking inspiration, or simply exploring the realms of imagination, I'm delighted to have you on this literary adventure.

Together, let's embark on a journey through the tapestry of words—a journey where stories unfold, characters come to life, and emotions dance in the spaces between sentences. Your curiosity, engagement, and enthusiasm bring vibrancy to the narratives, turning each piece into a collaborative creation.

Thank you for being a part of this community, and I invite you to immerse yourself in the stories that await. Feel free to share your thoughts, reflections, or embark on new adventures by suggesting topics. This space is a canvas where creativity and connection thrive.

Once again, welcome, and may the words written here resonate with you in unique and meaningful ways.

Happy reading!

# I'm Robin

The point of this story is to highlight the journey of a transgender individual named Lee, who later becomes Robin, and their pursuit of authenticity, self-acceptance, and advocacy for LGBTQ+ rights. The story emphasizes the challenges and triumphs faced by Robin as she navigates her identity, finds her voice, and uses her platform to create positive change.

Through Robin's experiences, the story aims to shed light on the importance of acceptance, inclusivity, and understanding for individuals of diverse gender identities and sexual orientations. It explores the struggles faced by transgender individuals, including the complexities of self-discovery, societal prejudice, and the courage required to live authentically.

Additionally, the story touches upon the significance of mentorship, community support, and allyship in the journey of self-actualization and the fight for equality. It emphasizes the transformative power of finding one's voice and using it to advocate for marginalized communities.

The story also raises awareness about the challenges faced by LGBTQ+ individuals in countries with less accepting attitudes and laws. It highlights the need for global solidarity, education, and advocacy to create a more inclusive world where everyone is treated with dignity and respect, regardless of their gender identity or sexual orientation.

Overall, the story intends to inspire empathy, promote understanding, and encourage individuals to stand up for equality and justice. It underscores the resilience and strength of those who persevere in the face of adversity, working towards a future where diversity is celebrated and all individuals can live authentically and without fear of discrimination.

The Story:
Once upon a time in the vibrant streets of Havana, Cuba, there lived a young and determined individual named Lee. Despite being assigned male at birth, Lee felt a deep longing within their heart to embrace their true identity as a female.

Lee had always been captivated by the heroic tales of Batman and his trusty sidekick, Robin. They admired Robin's courage, strength, and unwavering loyalty. Inspired by the iconic character, Lee dreamed of becoming the hero they knew they were meant to be.

However, Lee knew that their journey would not be easy. Cuba's society was deeply rooted in traditional norms, and the acceptance of gender diversity was still a work in progress. Lee understood that they would face numerous challenges and resistance along the way. But fueled by an unshakable spirit, Lee embarked on their quest for self-discovery and fulfillment.

Lee sought guidance and support from a few close friends who accepted and encouraged their true identity. They found solace in their creativity and began designing their own Robin-inspired outfit, tailored to reflect their unique personality. With each stitch, they felt a sense of empowerment and a step closer to their ultimate goal.

Word of Lee's aspiration spread throughout their neighborhood, and some people whispered disapprovingly. However, Lee's determination remained unswayed. They decided to seek out a mentor who could help them refine their skills and guide them on their path to becoming the hero they longed to be.

Through their relentless pursuit, Lee connected with an experienced female martial artist named Elena. She saw the fire in Lee's eyes and recognized their potential. Elena agreed to train Lee, teaching them various fighting techniques, acrobatics, and the virtues of bravery and honor.

Under Elena's watchful eye, Lee honed their physical abilities and built the mental resilience necessary to face the trials ahead. They grew stronger with each passing day, gaining confidence in their newfound skills and identity.

As Lee's training progressed, they couldn't help but notice the injustices within their community. Poverty and inequality plagued the streets of Havana, leaving many vulnerable and in need of a hero. Lee realized that they could make a difference, even before officially becoming Robin.

Donning their homemade Robin-inspired outfit, Lee began patrolling the city streets at night, intervening in situations where injustice prevailed. They protected the innocent, offered aid to the downtrodden, and stood up against oppressors, just as their hero would.

Despite initial skepticism, the people of Havana soon recognized Lee's selfless acts and unwavering dedication. The city embraced their presence and the symbol of hope they represented. Lee became an inspiration, breaking down the barriers of gender and demonstrating that true heroism knows no bounds.

Over time, Lee's transformation caught the attention of local media, sparking a nationwide conversation about acceptance, inclusivity, and the power of embracing one's authentic self. Through their own personal journey, Lee had become an emblem of resilience and bravery, encouraging others to embrace their own identities, whatever they may be.

As time went on, Lee's dream of becoming the official Robin gained momentum. Their story reached the ears of a renowned LGBTQ+ activist who saw the immense potential for change that Lee possessed. With their support and advocacy, Lee's dream became a reality.

Lee's gender transition process began, and they underwent various medical and psychological procedures to align their physical appearance with their true identity. Through it all, Lee remained resolute, knowing that the transformation would allow them to fully embody the hero they aspired to be.

Finally, as Lee stepped into the world as the female hero they had always envisioned, the people of Havana welcomed her with open arms. They celebrated her bravery, compassion, and unwavering

spirit. Lee had not only become the hero they yearned to be, but also a symbol of strength and acceptance for a nation on the cusp of change.

From that day forward, Lee, now known as Robin, continued to protect the streets of Havana, inspiring others to embrace their own unique identities and championing equality for all. With each leap, each swing from a rooftop, and each act of heroism, Robin left an indelible mark on the hearts and minds of

the Cuban people, reminding them that true heroism knows no boundaries and that the power to change the world lies within each individual, regardless of their gender or background.

As Robin continued her journey as a symbol of hope and equality in Havana, her impact expanded beyond the city's borders. News of her courageous acts and her own personal transformation spread throughout Cuba and reached international platforms.

Inspired by Robin's story, individuals from all walks of life began to question societal norms and challenge the constraints that limited their own self-expression. Robin's unwavering determination to live authentically resonated with people worldwide, sparking conversations about gender identity, acceptance, and the importance of embracing diversity.

Organizations dedicated to LGBTQ+ rights and gender equality recognized Robin's significant contributions and sought her partnership in their advocacy work. Together, they collaborated on initiatives aimed at promoting inclusivity and empowering individuals to be true to themselves, regardless of societal expectations.

As Robin's influence grew, she found herself traveling to different cities and countries, sharing her story and experiences with diverse audiences. She became a sought-after speaker at conferences, schools, and community gatherings, using her platform to educate, inspire, and encourage others to embrace their own personal journeys of self-discovery and acceptance.

Back in Havana, Robin's presence had a profound impact on the lives of LGBTQ+ youth who had struggled to find acceptance within their families and communities. Robin became a mentor figure, providing guidance, support, and a sense of belonging to those who felt marginalized.

In collaboration with local organizations, Robin helped establish support groups and safe spaces where individuals could come together, share their stories, and receive the support they needed. She became a beacon of hope for young people, assuring them that they were not alone and that their dreams and aspirations were valid.

Robin's impact reached the highest levels of government as well. Her story, combined with the growing demand for equality, compelled lawmakers to reassess existing policies and work toward enacting laws that protected the rights of transgender individuals. Robin's advocacy, along with the collective efforts of activists and allies, contributed to significant legal advancements, ensuring equal rights and protections for the LGBTQ+ community in Cuba.

But Robin's journey was not without its challenges. She faced backlash from conservative factions and individuals resistant to change. Yet, Robin remained resilient, fueled by the support and love she

received from her community and those whose lives she had touched. She knew that her mission was bigger than the obstacles in her path, and she pressed forward with unwavering determination.

As years passed, Robin's impact continued to ripple through Cuban society, fostering a more inclusive and accepting environment. Her legacy became intertwined with the history of Cuba's fight for equality, and her name became synonymous with courage, compassion, and the transformative power of embracing one's true self.

Lee, now fully embracing her identity as Robin, knew that her journey was far from over. With each new day, she remained committed to using her unique position to uplift others, create change, and inspire a world where every individual, regardless of their gender or background, could live authentically and without fear. And as she soared through the Cuban sky, Havana, and the world, knew that they had found their own real-life hero, reminding them that it is never too late to chase your dreams and make a difference in the world.

As time went on, Robin's impact extended beyond the boundaries of Cuba. Her story spread throughout the Latin American region and caught the attention of international organizations focused on human rights and LGBTQ+ advocacy.

Recognizing the power of Robin's journey, these organizations invited her to collaborate on global campaigns and initiatives. Robin became a prominent voice for transgender rights, traveling to different countries to share her experiences, promote inclusivity, and call for equal rights and protections for all individuals, regardless of their gender identity.

Through her activism, Robin connected with fellow transgender activists from around the world. Together, they formed a powerful network of change-makers, sharing strategies, resources, and support to amplify their collective voices and effect change on a global scale.

Robin's story inspired the creation of support networks and organizations in other countries, offering guidance, resources, and a sense of community for transgender individuals seeking acceptance and understanding. Her message of embracing one's true identity resonated deeply, prompting people from all walks of life to challenge societal norms and embrace the beauty of diversity.

Robin's journey also caught the attention of prominent figures in the entertainment industry. A renowned filmmaker was captivated by her story and sought to immortalize her heroic journey on the silver screen. The resulting film became an international sensation, further spreading awareness about transgender issues and challenging societal stereotypes.

With the film's success, Robin's advocacy gained even more momentum. She received invitations to speak at major conferences, including the United Nations, where she shared her insights and called for policy changes to protect the rights and well-being of transgender individuals worldwide.

Robin's unwavering dedication to her cause brought about tangible changes in legislation and social attitudes. Her advocacy, combined with the tireless efforts of countless individuals and organizations, led to significant advancements in transgender rights globally. Discrimination and prejudice began to recede, and more nations enacted laws to protect and support their transgender citizens.

Back in Cuba, Robin's impact on society was undeniable. Her story had sparked a cultural shift, fostering a greater understanding and acceptance of gender diversity. Schools began implementing comprehensive LGBTQ+ education programs, ensuring that future generations grew up with empathy, compassion, and respect for all individuals.

Robin's commitment to her community remained unwavering. She established the Robin Foundation, a nonprofit organization dedicated to providing resources, support, and mentorship for transgender individuals in Cuba and beyond. The foundation's programs included educational scholarships,

healthcare initiatives, and legal advocacy to ensure the rights and well-being of transgender individuals were protected.

As Robin continued her journey, she saw the transformative power of her own story and the collective efforts of countless individuals striving for equality. Her dream of becoming Robin, the hero she admired as a child, had evolved into something far greater—a beacon of hope and catalyst for change in the fight for equal rights and acceptance for transgender individuals worldwide.

And so, Robin's legacy endured, inspiring generations to come and reminding everyone that the pursuit of one's true identity and the quest for justice and equality were journeys worth embarking upon, no matter the challenges along the way.

As Robin's influence continued to spread, her advocacy work reached new heights. She collaborated with international human rights organizations, governments, and influential figures to push for systemic changes that would protect the rights and well-being of transgender individuals globally.

Through her efforts, Robin played a key role in the development and implementation of policies and legislation that ensured equal access to healthcare, education, employment, and legal protections for transgender individuals. Her tireless work contributed to the dismantling of discriminatory practices and the creation of a more inclusive society.

Robin also became a prominent figure in the fight against violence and discrimination targeting transgender individuals. She worked closely with organizations dedicated to combating hate crimes, promoting awareness, and fostering dialogue between communities, law enforcement agencies, and policymakers.

The impact of Robin's advocacy extended far beyond legislation. She utilized her platform to challenge societal misconceptions and stereotypes surrounding gender identity. Through public speaking engagements, media interviews, and social media, Robin engaged in candid conversations about transgender experiences, fostering empathy and understanding among broader audiences.

As her influence grew, Robin became an advisor and mentor to aspiring transgender activists, guiding them on their own journeys of advocacy and self-empowerment. She dedicated herself to building a network of resilient and passionate individuals who would carry the torch of transgender rights long into the future.

Recognizing the need for greater representation and visibility, Robin also ventured into the realm of entertainment and media. She collaborated with filmmakers, authors, and artists to ensure accurate and authentic portrayals of transgender characters and narratives in books, films, and television shows.

obin's story was adapted into a powerful documentary that shed light on the challenges faced by ansgender individuals and the importance of acceptance. The film received critical acclaim and won imerous awards, further raising awareness and sparking conversations about gender diversity on a obal scale.

hroughout her journey, Robin remained deeply connected to her roots in Cuba. She established ommunity centers and support networks throughout the country, providing vital resources, counseling rvices, and mentorship opportunities for transgender individuals. These safe spaces became hubs of npowerment and solidarity, fostering a sense of belonging and encouraging self-acceptance.

s the years went by, Robin's impact became an integral part of the fabric of Cuban society. Her lvocacy work and the progress achieved in transgender rights served as a testament to the power of erseverance, compassion, and the collective strength of a community united by a shared vision of quality.

obin's unwavering dedication and her ability to inspire change left an indelible mark on the world. er legacy continued to shape the lives of transgender individuals, fostering an environment where veryone could embrace their true selves without fear or judgment.

obin's story became a symbol of hope, reminding humanity of the transformative power of cceptance, compassion, and the unwavering belief in the inherent worth and dignity of every dividual. Her journey, from a young dreamer in Cuba to an internationally recognized advocate for ansgender rights, inspired countless others to break free from the shackles of societal expectations and ve authentically.

nd as Robin continued to champion the rights of transgender individuals, she knew that her work was ir from over. She remained dedicated to the ongoing fight for equality, determined to create a world here every person, regardless of their gender identity, could thrive, be celebrated, and contribute to a iore just and inclusive society.

he movie based on Robin's inspiring journey was titled "Wings of Authenticity." In the film, Robin rved as a consultant and played herself, bringing her own personal experiences and insights to the ory. Her role was pivotal in ensuring an authentic portrayal of the challenges, triumphs, and emotions iat transgender individuals face while navigating their identities and advocating for their rights.

Wings of Authenticity" became a critically acclaimed and influential film, shedding light on the ansgender experience and challenging societal norms and prejudices. Robin's participation in the iovie further elevated her platform and allowed her message of acceptance and equality to reach a roader audience, sparking important conversations about gender identity and inspiring positive change

ollowing the success of "Wings of Authenticity," Robin's involvement in the film industry expanded. he continued to collaborate with filmmakers and production companies, using her expertise and lived xperiences to shape narratives and bring greater authenticity to transgender characters and stories.

Robin took on various roles in subsequent films, not only as an actor but also as an advisor and advocate for transgender representation. She worked closely with directors and screenwriters, ensuring that transgender characters were portrayed respectfully and with depth, challenging stereotypes and promoting empathy.

Her contributions to the film industry extended beyond acting. Robin established her production company, dedicated to developing projects that centered on diverse and inclusive stories. She sought out emerging transgender filmmakers and provided mentorship and resources to help them share their unique perspectives on screen.

The films produced by Robin's company garnered critical acclaim, not only for their artistic merit but also for their contribution to changing the landscape of representation in the industry. Through these films, Robin continued to amplify transgender voices and stories, inspiring a new generation of filmmakers and challenging Hollywood to embrace diversity in all its forms.

Robin also became a sought-after speaker and panelist at film festivals and industry events, sharing her expertise on transgender representation and advocating for greater inclusivity within the entertainment world. Her powerful speeches and discussions influenced filmmakers, producers, and executives, encouraging them to actively seek out diverse voices and stories that reflect the richness of human experiences.

Outside of the film industry, Robin remained an unwavering advocate for transgender rights. She leveraged her platform to address systemic issues, collaborate with policymakers, and promote legislative changes that would protect transgender individuals from discrimination and ensure their equal rights under the law.

Robin's tireless efforts garnered international recognition. She received prestigious awards for her activism, both within the film industry and the broader human rights community. Her influence reached beyond borders as she became a global ambassador for transgender rights, speaking at international conferences and engaging in dialogues with world leaders to promote greater acceptance and equality for all individuals.

While Robin's journey in the film industry and activism continued to evolve, she never lost sight of her roots in Cuba. She maintained a strong connection to her community, providing ongoing support to transgender individuals in the country and collaborating with local organizations to advance transgender rights and well-being.

Through her multifaceted work, Robin inspired countless individuals to embrace their authentic selves and strive for a more inclusive world. Her impact on the film industry and the global fight for transgender rights was immeasurable, leaving a lasting legacy of compassion, resilience, and positive change.

Early years:

In the early years of her journey, before embracing her identity as Robin, she found work at a popular club in Havana as a female impersonator. With her striking looks and captivating stage presence, Robin quickly gained a reputation for her exceptional talent and became a local sensation.

As a female impersonator, Robin honed her skills in performing arts, mastering the art of transforming herself into glamorous female personas. Her performances showcased her creativity, versatility, and ability to captivate audiences with her charisma and stage presence.

Robin's fame as a female impersonator extended beyond the borders of Cuba. Travelers from different parts of the world flocked to the club to witness her captivating performances. She became a sought-after entertainer, often headlining shows and attracting a loyal fan base.

While Robin's success as a female impersonator brought her recognition and adoration, it also provided her with a unique platform to challenge societal norms and spark conversations about gender

identity. Her performances blurred the lines between traditional gender roles, inspiring audiences to question preconceived notions and embrace the fluidity and complexity of human expression.

Robin's experiences as a female impersonator were instrumental in shaping her understanding of gender identity and the power of performance as a means of self-expression. It was during this time that she began to question her own journey and the possibility of living her life authentically as a transgender woman.

As Robin's fame grew, so did her aspirations to use her platform for more than entertainment. She recognized the potential to bring about meaningful change and empowerment for transgender individuals, both within and outside the realm of performance.

It was this realization that eventually led Robin to embark on her transformative journey, shedding her role as a female impersonator and embracing her true identity as Robin—a beacon of hope and a powerful advocate for transgender rights. Her experiences as a performer continued to inform her activism, reminding her of the power of visibility, representation, and self-expression in challenging societal norms and fostering acceptance.

Robin's time as a famous female impersonator served as a significant chapter in her life, propelling her towards her ultimate purpose as a trailblazing transgender activist and advocate. It was through her experiences on the stage that she discovered her own strength, resilience, and the capacity to inspire change on a larger scale.

Indeed, Robin's performances as a female impersonator showcased her exceptional talent and versatility. On stage, she flawlessly embodied a variety of iconic figures and celebrities, captivating audiences with her transformative portrayals and undeniable stage presence.

As Robin stepped into the spotlight, she mesmerized audiences with her portrayal of Tina Turner, capturing the powerhouse vocals, electrifying dance moves, and undeniable charisma of the legendary performer. Her dynamic performances of Tina's hits brought the crowd to their feet, singing along and reveling in the energy she exuded on stage.

With her uncanny ability to capture the essence of different artists, Robin also took on the persona of Cher, mesmerizing audiences with her renditions of Cher's greatest hits. From the distinctive voice to the glamorous costumes, she flawlessly channeled the iconic singer, earning applause and admiration for her attention to detail.

Whitney Houston's timeless songs became another highlight of Robin's repertoire. Her breathtaking vocals and emotional delivery transported audiences back to the iconic performances of the late diva. As Robin brought Whitney's songs to life, her powerful voice soared through the venue, leaving an indelible impression on all who witnessed her heartfelt renditions.

Beyond Tina Turner, Cher, and Whitney Houston, Robin also delved into portraying other beloved figures from the world of entertainment. From Madonna's rebellious spirit to Marilyn Monroe's timeless allure, Robin's performances celebrated the diversity of talent and charisma that defined these cultural icons.

Her ability to embody these characters with such authenticity and passion set her apart as a truly exceptional performer. Audiences were captivated by her stage presence, talent, and the way she paid homage to these legendary figures while also infusing her own unique style and energy into each performance.

Robin's popularity as a female impersonator skyrocketed as word of her incredible talent spread. Her shows became must-see events, drawing in audiences from all walks of life who were eager to witness her remarkable transformations and experience the magic she created on stage.

While her success as a female impersonator brought her fame and adoration, it also provided Robin with a powerful platform to challenge societal norms and promote inclusivity. Through her performances, she encouraged audiences to embrace the beauty of diversity and celebrate the freedom of self-expression.

As Robin's journey progressed, she would transition from the realm of entertainment to becoming a leading advocate for transgender rights. Her experiences as a famous female impersonator would shape her understanding of the transformative power of performance and prepare her for the impactful role she would play in promoting acceptance and equality for transgender individuals worldwide.

As Robin's journey continued to unfold, fate brought her into the path of Diana, a young and aspiring drag queen who had a burning desire to learn and grow in the art of performance. Recognizing Diana's potential and determination, Robin took it upon herself to become her mentor and guide, sharing her knowledge, experiences, and wisdom.

Robin saw a reflection of her own journey in Diana and understood the importance of providing support and guidance to those who aspired to express their true selves through the art of drag. She recognized that drag, like her own experiences as a female impersonator, had the power to challenge norms and create spaces of empowerment and self-expression.

Under Robin's guidance, Diana began to blossom as a performer. Robin shared her expertise in stage presence, vocal technique, costume design, and the nuances of character portrayal. She emphasized the importance of authenticity, encouraging Diana to embrace her unique identity and infuse it into her performances.

Beyond the technical aspects, Robin also nurtured Diana's self-confidence and self-acceptance. She provided emotional support and reassurance, reminding Diana that true artistry stems from staying true to oneself. Together, they explored the power of storytelling through drag, using their performances to shed light on important social issues and spark conversations about acceptance, equality, and the beauty of diversity.

Their mentor-mentee relationship grew into a strong bond built on trust, mutual respect, and shared aspirations. Robin not only taught Diana the skills of the trade but also instilled in her a sense of responsibility as a performer—to use her platform to uplift others and advocate for positive change.

As Diana developed her own unique style and voice, she began to perform alongside Robin, bringing their collaborative performances to stages across Cuba and beyond. Their dynamic chemistry and

complementary talents captivated audiences, inspiring others to embrace their true selves and find their own creative outlets for self-expression.

Together, Robin and Diana became a dynamic duo, using their performances to challenge societal norms, break down barriers, and spread messages of love, acceptance, and equality. They became beacons of hope for the LGBTQ+ community, showcasing the power of unity and the transformative potential of art to create positive social change.

As their impact grew, Robin and Diana also dedicated themselves to mentoring other aspiring drag queens, creating a supportive community that nurtured talent and encouraged individual growth. They hosted workshops and events, providing a platform for emerging performers to showcase their skills and find their voices.

Through their mentorship, Robin and Diana sought to create a legacy of empowered performers who would continue to push boundaries, inspire others, and advocate for LGBTQ+ rights. Their collaboration not only transformed the lives of those they mentored but also contributed to a more inclusive and accepting society.

Together, Robin and Diana became a force to be reckoned with, using their artistry and mentorship to shape a future where individuals could express their true selves without fear, celebrate their uniqueness, and promote a world where love and acceptance reigned supreme

As their mentorship journey continued, Robin and Diana recognized the importance of supporting and uplifting other aspiring drag queens who were seeking guidance and encouragement. They saw the potential to create a strong community of talented performers who could inspire one another and collectively promote acceptance, creativity, and self-expression.

Together, Robin and Diana organized regular mentorship programs and workshops specifically tailored to the needs of aspiring drag queens. These programs provided a safe and inclusive space where individuals could explore their artistic identities, develop their skills, and gain confidence in their abilities.

During the mentorship programs, Robin and Diana shared their knowledge and experiences, covering various aspects of drag performance such as makeup techniques, costume design, stage presence, and character development. They emphasized the importance of authenticity, self-acceptance, and embracing individuality.

The mentorship sessions also focused on the emotional and personal aspects of being a drag queen. Robin and Diana provided guidance on navigating challenges, building resilience, and overcoming obstacles that may arise on the journey to self-expression. They fostered a supportive environment where participants could freely discuss their experiences, fears, and aspirations, offering encouragement and understanding.

In addition to the mentorship programs, Robin and Diana organized showcases and performance opportunities for the mentees to exhibit their talents and connect with the wider drag community. These events served as platforms for emerging drag queens to gain exposure, receive feedback, and establish valuable connections within the industry.

The mentorship extended beyond the workshop sessions and performances. Robin and Diana made themselves available as ongoing sources of support, offering guidance, advice, and a listening ear to their mentees. They understood the transformative power of having a mentor and recognized the importance of building a strong network of support within the drag community.

Through their dedication to mentoring, Robin and Diana nurtured a new generation of drag queens who were empowered to embrace their true selves, push boundaries, and use their artistry as a catalyst for social change. The mentees not only developed their skills and craft but also grew into confident advocates for LGBTQ+ rights and acceptance.

The impact of Robin and Diana's mentorship programs extended far beyond the individual mentees. By fostering a sense of community and supporting the growth of emerging drag queens, they contributed to the overall visibility and recognition of drag as an art form. Their efforts helped challenge stereotypes, break down barriers, and promote understanding and acceptance in society at large.

The legacy of Robin and Diana's mentorship programs lives on, with their mentees going on to become mentors themselves, creating a continuous cycle of support, guidance, and inspiration within the drag community. Through their collective efforts, they have created a vibrant, inclusive, and empowering environment where aspiring drag queens can find their voices, embrace their identities, and make their mark on the world of performance.

As Robin continued her mentorship programs and empowered countless young individuals within the drag community, she encountered a bittersweet turn of events when Diana, her mentee and dear friend, got married and chose to step away from the world of drag.

lthough Robin felt a sense of loss when Diana left, she understood and respected her friend's decision. ife takes unexpected turns, and priorities can shift. Robin remained grateful for the time they had ared, the impact they had made together, and the growth they had witnessed in one another.

hile Diana's departure left a void, Robin decided to forge ahead and carry on with her work. She derstood that her journey as a mentor was not dependent on one individual but rather on the llective impact she could have on the lives of many.

ith renewed determination and a deep sense of purpose, Robin continued to mentor aspiring drag ueens, investing her energy, knowledge, and love into shaping the next generation of performers. She mained steadfast in her belief that mentorship could be a catalyst for personal growth, self-cceptance, and positive change.

obin expanded her mentorship programs, reaching out to more individuals who were hungry for uidance and support. She created platforms for emerging drag queens to showcase their talents, ganized workshops, and established a strong community where mentorship, collaboration, and elebration thrived.

hrough her continued efforts, Robin became an influential figure in the drag community, admired for er talent, resilience, and commitment to uplifting others. Her mentorship programs gave young

eople hope, providing them with a sense of belonging and the tools to navigate their own journeys of elf-discovery.

eyond her role as a mentor, Robin continued to blaze trails as a performer. Her captivating stage resence, powerful vocals, and mesmerizing transformations captivated audiences worldwide. She used er platform to amplify important social messages, advocate for LGBTQ+ rights, and challenge cietal norms.

obin's impact extended beyond the drag community. She became a symbol of resilience and npowerment, inspiring individuals from all walks of life to embrace their authentic selves and live ith courage and conviction. Her story of perseverance and success resonated with people around the orld, and she became a beacon of hope for those facing adversity.

s Robin continued to mentor, perform, and advocate for equality, her influence grew exponentially. he received recognition and accolades for her contributions to the arts and LGBTQ+ activism, lidifying her position as an icon and role model.

obin's journey, shaped by her experiences as a mentor and performer, propelled her to become a ailblazer in the drag community and an advocate for marginalized voices. Through her unwavering ommitment to authenticity, inclusivity, and mentorship, she transformed herself into an influential rce, leaving an indelible mark on the world of drag and inspiring generations to come

obin's extraordinary journey as a mentor, performer, and advocate caught the attention of filmmakers ho recognized the power and significance of her story. As a result, her life and experiences became the subject of a powerful documentary that aimed to shed light on the challenges faced by transgender individuals and emphasize the vital importance of acceptance.

The documentary, titled "Beyond the Mirror: Robin's Story," delved deep into Robin's personal journey chronicling her transformation from a young individual seeking to express her true self to a trailblazing figure in the drag community and a prominent advocate for transgender rights.

The film captured the highs and lows of Robin's life, revealing the triumphs and challenges she faced along the way. It explored her early years in Cuba, her emergence as a renowned female impersonator, her mentorship of aspiring drag queens, and her unwavering commitment to promoting acceptance and equality.

"Beyond the Mirror: Robin's Story" went beyond a mere biographical account, delving into the broader issues surrounding transgender identity and the struggles faced by individuals within the LGBTQ+ community. It featured interviews with Robin's mentees, friends, and fellow activists, who shared their perspectives on the transformative impact of Robin's mentorship and her unwavering dedication to advocating for transgender rights.

The documentary also gave a voice to other transgender individuals, highlighting their stories, struggles, and triumphs, in order to create a comprehensive narrative that fostered understanding, empathy, and inclusivity. It explored the societal challenges and prejudices faced by transgender people and aimed to inspire viewers to embrace diversity, challenge stereotypes, and foster a more accepting world.

"Beyond the Mirror: Robin's Story" received critical acclaim and became a catalyst for important conversations about gender identity, acceptance, and the power of mentorship. It premiered at prestigious film festivals, garnering accolades and capturing the hearts of audiences worldwide.

The documentary's impact extended far beyond the screen, as it sparked meaningful dialogue and motivated individuals to become agents of change in their own communities. Its message of compassion and acceptance resonated with people from all walks of life, fostering empathy and understanding for transgender individuals and the challenges they face.

Through "Beyond the Mirror: Robin's Story," Robin's journey became an emblematic representation of the broader struggles and triumphs of the transgender community. Her story illuminated the transformative power of mentorship, the strength of self-acceptance, and the profound impact one individual can have in promoting inclusivity and social change.

Ultimately, the documentary played a significant role in raising awareness, fostering empathy, and inspiring action to create a world where transgender individuals are embraced, celebrated, and afforded the dignity and respect they deserve

The Past:
In the late 1970s, just before Lee embarked on her transformative journey to become Robin, she carried with her a dark past, a collection of experiences that shaped her in profound ways. These experiences,

though challenging and difficult, would ultimately become catalysts for her growth, resilience, and determination to create a better future for herself and others.

As Lee, she had faced numerous struggles and obstacles in a society that often lacked understanding and acceptance of transgender individuals. She grappled with feelings of confusion, isolation, and the fear of being rejected for her true identity. Lee's early years were marked by a deep internal struggle as she navigated her gender identity while attempting to find her place in the world.

During this period, Lee faced discrimination, harassment, and a lack of support. She encountered situations that tested her strength and resilience, pushing her to confront her darkest moments head-on. These experiences, though painful, would ultimately ignite a fire within her—a determination to overcome adversity and pave the way for a more inclusive society.

Lee's dark past involved instances of discrimination, prejudice, and even violence. She had experienced moments of fear and vulnerability, grappling with societal pressures and expectations that sought to stifle her true self. These challenges served as a stark reminder of the urgent need for change, fueling Lee's resolve to rise above her circumstances and create a better future.

Amidst the darkness, Lee found glimmers of hope and strength. She encountered allies who offered support and understanding, providing glimpses of acceptance and possibility. These individuals became beacons of light in Lee's life, reinforcing her belief that there was a brighter path ahead, waiting to be forged.

It was during this transformative period that Lee made the decision to embark on a journey of self-discovery and transformation. She embraced her true identity as Robin, a name symbolizing rebirth and newfound purpose. With each step forward, Robin carried the weight of her past experiences,

using them as a driving force to advocate for change, inspire others, and build a future where transgender individuals could live authentically and without fear.

Robin's dark past became an integral part of her story—a testament to her resilience, determination, and unwavering spirit. As she emerged from the shadows, she carried within her a profound understanding of the challenges faced by transgender individuals, and a fierce commitment to create a more inclusive and accepting world.

Her journey from Lee to Robin would become a source of inspiration for countless others who found solace, strength, and hope in her story. Robin's dark past, once a burden, became a catalyst for her transformation and the driving force behind her unwavering dedication to advocacy, mentorship, and the pursuit of a more accepting society

After Diana's departure, Robin felt a profound sense of loss and missed her dear friend immensely. The bond they had forged through their shared passion for drag and mentorship was a significant part of Robin's life. However, even in Diana's absence, Robin found solace and comfort in her work as a performer and mentor.

As Robin continued to pour her heart and soul into her performances, she discovered that the stage became a sanctuary—a place where she could express herself fully and channel her emotions into her art. Each time she stepped into the spotlight, she felt a renewed sense of purpose and connection to her audience.

Through her performances, Robin was able to honor her own journey while inspiring others who may be going through similar experiences. She used her platform to raise awareness about the challenges faced by transgender individuals, fostering understanding and empathy within her audience.

Robin's work as a mentor also provided her with a sense of fulfillment and purpose. She dedicated herself to guiding and supporting aspiring drag queens, just as she had done with Diana. Witnessing the growth and success of her mentees brought her immense joy and served as a reminder of the positive impact she was making in their lives.

While the void left by Diana's absence was still present, Robin learned to find strength within herself and in the community she had built. She surrounded herself with fellow drag performers, friends, and allies who provided support and understanding during difficult times. Their unwavering encouragement helped Robin navigate the emotional rollercoaster of missing Diana.

In the process, Robin discovered her own resilience and inner power. She realized that she possessed the strength to continue her journey, pursuing her dreams and creating a lasting impact in the drag community and beyond.

Robin's dedication to her work became a form of self-care and healing. It allowed her to channel her emotions, celebrate her identity, and contribute to a larger cause of promoting acceptance and inclusivity. Through her performances and mentorship, Robin found purpose, inspiration, and a renewed sense of hope.

While the absence of Diana remained a poignant reminder of their time together, Robin's love for her friend was transformed into a driving force—a reminder to cherish and embrace the connections she

had in her life. And through her continued work, Robin ensured that Diana's legacy lived on, inspiring future generations of performers and mentors.

In the end, Robin's commitment to her art and mentorship became a source of strength, helping her navigate the complexities of loss and finding fulfillment in her own unique journey. She remained grateful for the time she had shared with Diana, cherishing the memories and lessons they had learned together, while forging ahead with determination, resilience, and a heart filled with love.

One day, fueled by her adventurous spirit and a desire to explore new horizons, Robin made the decision to embark on a trip to Russia. Excitement coursed through her veins as she envisioned immersing herself in the rich culture, history, and vibrant LGBTQ+ community she had heard about.

However, as Robin arrived in Russia, she quickly realized that the reality on the ground was different from her expectations. The country's social and political climate posed significant challenges for LGBTQ+ individuals, with widespread discrimination and hostility.

Robin encountered difficulties from the moment she set foot in Russia. She faced prejudice and intolerance, experiencing firsthand the harsh realities many LGBTQ+ individuals faced in their daily lives. From subtle acts of discrimination to overt hostility, Robin found herself navigating an environment that seemed unwelcoming and even dangerous.

Her attempts to connect with local LGBTQ+ communities were met with caution and fear. Many individuals she met had experienced discrimination, violence, and had to hide their true identities for their own safety. It was a stark reminder of the struggles faced by marginalized communities in societies that lacked acceptance and legal protections.

Despite the challenging circumstances, Robin remained resilient and determined to make a positive impact. She sought opportunities to connect with local activists and organizations, offering support and solidarity in their fight for LGBTQ+ rights. Together, they shared stories, experiences, and strategies to advocate for change and foster greater acceptance.

Robin's trip to Russia became a profound learning experience. She witnessed firsthand the power of resilience and the importance of global solidarity in the face of adversity. Her interactions with local LGBTQ+ activists and individuals inspired her to continue using her platform to raise awareness, challenge stereotypes, and advocate for equality.

While her journey in Russia was not without its difficulties, Robin's presence and engagement had a lasting impact. By sharing her own story and listening to the stories of others, she helped foster understanding and empathy within the communities she encountered.

Ultimately, Robin's trip to Russia became a catalyst for change, both within herself and in the broader LGBTQ+ movement. It reinforced her commitment to using her platform to amplify marginalized voices, advocate for equal rights, and create spaces of inclusivity wherever she went.

Though her trip to Russia may have presented challenges, it only served to strengthen Robin's resolve. She returned home with a renewed determination to continue her work, knowing that her experiences and interactions in Russia had deepened her understanding of the global struggle for LGBTQ+ rights.

Robin's journey taught her that even in the face of adversity, unity, compassion, and resilience could spark change. Her trip to Russia became a pivotal chapter in her story, reminding her of the urgency and significance of her advocacy efforts and fueling her commitment to creating a world where everyone, regardless of their sexual orientation or gender identity, can live with dignity, acceptance, and equality.

Robin's outspoken support for LGBTQ+ rights attracted the attention of the authorities. Her boldness in challenging the prevailing attitudes and advocating for equality put her in a precarious situation.

Robin's arrest sent shockwaves through the LGBTQ+ community and garnered international attention. News of her incarceration spread rapidly, sparking outrage and drawing global scrutiny towards Russia's treatment of LGBTQ+ individuals. Activists, organizations, and human rights advocates rallied together, using Robin's case as a rallying point to call for change and raise awareness about the violations of LGBTQ+ rights.

During her three-week imprisonment, Robin endured hardships and faced the harsh realities of the justice system. However, her spirit remained unbroken, and she found solace in the support and solidarity pouring in from around the world. Letters of encouragement, demonstrations of solidarity, and international pressure mounted, putting pressure on Russian authorities to release her.

Robin's imprisonment, though a dark and challenging period in her life, served as a catalyst for renewed determination and amplified her voice as a passionate advocate. Her story became a symbol of resilience and sparked a global conversation about the importance of defending LGBTQ+ rights and challenging oppressive regimes.

Upon her release, Robin's return to her community was met with an outpouring of support and celebration. Her courage and sacrifice in the face of adversity elevated her status as a respected and influential figure in the LGBTQ+ movement.

Robin continued her activism, using her experience in Russia to shed light on the human rights abuses and discrimination faced by LGBTQ+ individuals worldwide. She became an even stronger advocate, leveraging her platform to advocate for policy changes, educate others, and promote dialogue to foster acceptance and equality.

Through her resilience and unwavering dedication, Robin inspired countless individuals to stand up for their rights and work towards a more inclusive world. Her story, and the international attention it garnered, contributed to ongoing efforts to challenge discriminatory practices and advance LGBTQ+ rights both in Russia and globally.

After her release from imprisonment in Russia, Robin's determination to fight for LGBTQ+ rights only grew stronger. She channeled her experiences into a renewed commitment to advocate for equality, both in her home country and on the international stage.

Robin's story became widely known, and she was invited to share her experiences at conferences, rallies, and human rights events around the world. Her powerful speeches captivated audiences, drawing attention to the ongoing challenges faced by LGBTQ+ individuals in Russia and beyond.

Motivated by her own ordeal, Robin dedicated herself to strengthening alliances with LGBTQ+ organizations and activists globally. She collaborated with international human rights groups to develop strategies for effecting change, fostering unity among LGBTQ+ communities worldwide.

Recognizing the importance of education and awareness, Robin spearheaded campaigns to promote understanding and acceptance of LGBTQ+ individuals. Through public speaking engagements, media interviews, and social media platforms, she worked tirelessly to dispel stereotypes, challenge prejudice, and create a safer, more inclusive environment for all.

Robin's efforts were not limited to advocacy alone. She established a foundation to provide resources and support to LGBTQ+ individuals in need, particularly those facing discrimination, violence, or unjust treatment. The foundation offered counseling, legal aid, and community programs to empower individuals and promote their well-being.

s Robin continued her work, she found allies in influential figures from various sectors—ntertainment, politics, and human rights—who recognized the importance of her cause. Collaborations ith celebrities, politicians, and influential organizations further amplified her message, reaching wider idiences and inspiring greater support for LGBTQ+ rights.

obin's impact extended beyond the boundaries of activism. She became a symbol of hope for ountless individuals struggling with their own identities and facing adversity due to societal prejudice. hrough her authenticity, resilience, and unwavering commitment, she showed that it was possible to vercome obstacles and create positive change.

ver time, the momentum generated by Robin's advocacy efforts began to produce tangible results. Her ory, along with the collective efforts of countless activists, led to increased international pressure on ie Russian government to address human rights violations and enact legal protections for LGBTQ+ idividuals.

Jhile progress was gradual, Robin remained steadfast in her pursuit of a more just and inclusive ociety. Her dedication to the cause resonated with others, inspiring a new generation of activists to ontinue the fight for LGBTQ+ rights long after she was gone.

ears later, Robin's legacy lived on, not only through the legal changes achieved but also in the hearts id minds of those she touched. Her story became an integral part of the LGBTQ+ movement's history, testament to the power of resilience, advocacy, and the belief in a world where everyone is treated ith dignity and equality.

s time went on, Robin's impact continued to reverberate, ensuring that her advocacy and the xperiences she endured in Russia would never be forgotten. Her journey became a source of ispiration, reminding individuals of the importance of standing up for what is right, even in the face of dversity.

nd so, Robin's story serves as a reminder that no matter the obstacles faced, the fight for equality and istice is worth every effort. Through her passion, determination, and unwavering belief in the power f change, she played a significant role in shaping a more inclusive and accepting world for LGBTQ+ idividuals everywhere.

# Mystery in Costa Rica

Once upon a time, in the beautiful land of Costa Rica, there lived a couple deeply in love. Their name were Maria and Alejandro. They had always dreamt of building a life together, filled with love, laughter, and a family of their own.

As the years passed, Maria and Alejandro's love grew stronger, and their desire to have children became more profound. They dreamt of watching their children play on the sandy beaches and exploring the lush rainforests of their homeland.

However, despite their efforts and numerous attempts, Maria was unable to conceive. They visited doctors and sought medical advice, but the news was disheartening. Maria had a medical condition th made it difficult for her to get pregnant.

Though saddened by this news, Maria and Alejandro didn't let despair consume them. They were determined to find happiness in other ways. They dedicated their lives to exploring the beauty of Cost Rica together, nurturing their love, and embracing the joys of life.

One day, while Maria and Alejandro were hiking through the dense rainforest, they stumbled upon a small, abandoned animal shelter. Curiosity led them inside, and they discovered a variety of animals i need of care and love. Their hearts melted at the sight of the adorable creatures.

Maria and Alejandro's love for each other extended to all living beings. They decided to volunteer at the shelter, devoting their time and efforts to providing a safe haven for the animals. They nurtured th injured, fed the hungry, and showered them with endless love.

Months turned into years as Maria and Alejandro's lives revolved around their newfound purpose. The found solace in helping these animals, cherishing the love and gratitude they received in return. Their hearts were filled with joy, even though their dream of having their own children hadn't come to fruition.

Then, one sunny morning, a heartwarming surprise awaited them at the shelter. A distressed employee approached Maria and Alejandro, holding a tiny bundle wrapped in a soft blanket. They were both surprised and confused.

The employee smiled warmly and explained that a rare species of monkey, native to the rainforests of Costa Rica, had been orphaned. Due to unforeseen circumstances, the shelter was unable to find a suitable habitat for the baby monkey. They knew Maria and Alejandro's love for animals and their commitment to the shelter, so they asked if they would be willing to adopt the little one.

Maria and Alejandro looked at each other, their eyes brimming with tears of joy. The sweet surprise they had been given wasn't what they had expected, but it was a gift that would forever change their lives. They agreed without hesitation, feeling an instant connection to the little monkey.

They named her Esperanza, which means "hope" in Spanish. Esperanza brought immeasurable joy into Maria and Alejandro's lives. She became the child they had longed for, filling their days with laughter, mischief, and unconditional love.

The family of three continued to care for the animals at the shelter, and their love story spread far and wide. People from all corners of the world were inspired by their compassion and dedication. Maria and Alejandro became renowned for their work in animal conservation, and their efforts helped protect the rich biodiversity of Costa Rica's rainforests.

Though they had faced challenges on their journey to parenthood, Maria and Alejandro's love transcended conventional expectations. Their love for each other, the animals, and the natural beauty of their homeland blossomed, creating a life more extraordinary than they could have ever imagined.

And so, Maria, Alejandro, and little Esperanza lived happily ever after, surrounded by the enchanting beauty of Costa Rica, and their hearts forever grateful for the sweet surprise that changed their lives in ways they had never dreamed possible.

As the years passed, Maria, Alejandro, and Esperanza continued to thrive in their life together. The shelter they had once stumbled upon grew and flourished, becoming a sanctuary for various endangered species in Costa Rica. The couple's dedication to animal conservation had inspired many others to join their cause, and together, they made a significant impact in protecting the country's unique wildlife.

As Esperanza grew older, she became an ambassador for her species. Maria and Alejandro, with Esperanza by their side, traveled across Costa Rica, visiting schools, communities, and even international conferences to raise awareness about the importance of preserving the rainforests and the creatures that call them home.

Esperanza's story touched the hearts of many, and people were captivated by her playful nature and her deep bond with Maria and Alejandro. The trio became local celebrities, featuring in documentaries and news articles that showcased their extraordinary journey and the impact they were making.

Their work caught the attention of a renowned wildlife organization, and they were invited to collaborate on a groundbreaking project. The organization was planning to establish a wildlife rehabilitation center in a remote part of Costa Rica, aiming to rescue and rehabilitate animals affected by deforestation and illegal trade. Maria and Alejandro's expertise and passion made them the perfect candidates to lead the project.

Eager to contribute to this important initiative, Maria, Alejandro, and Esperanza embraced the opportunity wholeheartedly. They dedicated themselves to building a state-of-the-art facility, assembling a team of skilled veterinarians and conservationists who shared their vision.

Once the rehabilitation center was complete, animals from all corners of the country found solace within its walls. Maria and Alejandro worked tirelessly, ensuring that each creature received the care, attention, and chance at a better life they deserved. They witnessed countless success stories as injured animals were nursed back to health and released into protected habitats.

The rehabilitation center soon became a symbol of hope for Costa Rica's wildlife. It attracted volunteers from around the world, who joined forces with Maria, Alejandro, and their team to create a brighter future for the country's threatened species.

Years turned into decades, and Maria and Alejandro's legacy as champions of animal conservation grew stronger with time. Their dedication to each other, their love for the natural world, and the unexpected arrival of Esperanza had propelled them into a life of purpose and fulfillment.

As they reached the twilight of their lives, Maria and Alejandro passed on their knowledge and passion to the next generation of conservationists. Their story became an integral part of Costa Rica's history, inspiring countless individuals to protect the planet's biodiversity and preserve the love that binds humans and animals together.

And so, the tale of Maria, Alejandro, and Esperanza lives on, echoing through the rainforests of Costa Rica as a testament to the power of love, resilience, and the extraordinary journeys that unfold when we embrace life's sweet surprises.

In the final chapter of their remarkable story, Maria and Alejandro decided to retire from their active roles in the wildlife rehabilitation center, passing the torch to the capable hands they had mentored over the years. They transitioned into a quieter life, surrounded by the tranquility of Costa Rica's natural wonders.

With their newfound free time, Maria and Alejandro embarked on a personal journey of exploration and reflection. They traveled to different regions of Costa Rica, immersing themselves in its diverse ecosystems and connecting with the rhythms of nature. They visited breathtaking waterfalls, serene beaches, and hidden gems tucked away in the lush rainforests.

During their travels, they encountered communities deeply rooted in traditional practices and sustainable living. Inspired by their encounters, Maria and Alejandro felt a deep calling to contribute further to the preservation of Costa Rica's cultural heritage alongside its natural beauty.

They partnered with local indigenous communities, learning from their wisdom and supporting their efforts to protect their ancestral lands. Together, they worked on initiatives that focused on sustainable agriculture, cultural revitalization, and eco-tourism, ensuring that future generations would continue to cherish and respect the country's rich heritage.

As their love continued to deepen over the years, Maria and Alejandro cherished every moment spent together. They often reminisced about their journey, marveling at how their lives had unfolded, guided by love, compassion, and the unwavering belief in the power of unexpected surprises.

In the twilight of their lives, Maria and Alejandro found solace in nurturing their relationship and spending time with their extended family. The shelter they had established so long ago remained a thriving testament to their devotion, carrying on their legacy of protecting Costa Rica's precious wildlife.

Surrounded by the love of their children, grandchildren, and great-grandchildren, Maria and Alejandro's hearts were filled with joy and contentment. Their story had become an integral part of their family's history, passed down through generations as a reminder of the extraordinary things that can happen when we embrace life's twists and turns with an open heart.

When the time came for Maria and Alejandro to bid farewell to this earthly realm, they left behind a legacy that would forever inspire others to protect and cherish the natural world. Their love story in

Costa Rica became a timeless tale, etched in the hearts of those who heard it, reminding them of the transformative power of love, resilience, and the magic that lies hidden within life's unexpected surprises.

And so, their spirits danced among the vibrant rainforests and shimmering beaches of Costa Rica, forever entwined in the tapestry of a land that had embraced their love and passion for all living beings. Their story lives on, a testament to the profound connection between two souls, the beauty of nature, and the extraordinary impact one couple can have on the world around them.

In the years that followed, the tale of Maria and Alejandro's love and their dedication to the preservation of Costa Rica's natural and cultural heritage continued to resonate with people around the

world. Their story was immortalized in books, documentaries, and even a heartwarming feature film that touched the hearts of millions.

The film captured the essence of their love, their journey, and their unwavering commitment to making a difference. Audiences were moved by the beauty of Costa Rica and the profound impact that a single couple could have on the lives of animals, communities, and the planet itself.

As the film gained recognition and accolades, Maria and Alejandro became celebrated figures not only in Costa Rica but on an international scale. They were invited to speak at global conferences and events, sharing their wisdom, experiences, and inspiring others to take action for the preservation of our planet.

Moved by their story, philanthropists and environmental organizations extended their support to the causes Maria and Alejandro held dear. Donations poured in, providing resources to expand the reach of their initiatives, protect more habitats, and support sustainable practices.

With the newfound resources, Maria and Alejandro's vision expanded further. They collaborated with other countries and organizations to implement similar wildlife conservation and cultural preservation projects around the globe. Their love had become a catalyst for change on a global scale.

Even in their later years, Maria and Alejandro remained active in their efforts, traveling the world to lend their expertise and support to various conservation initiatives. Their unwavering dedication inspired a new generation of environmentalists, who followed in their footsteps and carried on their legacy of love and preservation.

As time went on, Maria and Alejandro's health began to falter, but their spirits remained strong. They took solace in knowing that their life's work had made a significant impact and that their love had touched countless lives.

When the time came for Maria and Alejandro to depart this world, they did so surrounded by their loved ones and with hearts full of gratitude. Their passing was mourned by many, but their memory lived on as a beacon of hope and inspiration.

In honor of their remarkable journey, a foundation was established in their names, dedicated to continuing their work in wildlife conservation, cultural preservation, and fostering love for the planet. The foundation became a hub of innovation, bringing together scientists, educators, and activists who shared Maria and Alejandro's vision.

Generations to come would learn about their story, drawing inspiration from their love, resilience, and their unyielding belief in the power of individuals to create positive change. Their legacy would forever be etched in the annals of history, serving as a reminder that love, coupled with passion and action, has the power to shape the world in extraordinary ways.

And so, the tale of Maria and Alejandro, two souls united in love, left an indelible mark on the hearts and minds of people everywhere. Their story reminds us that even in the face of adversity, with love as our compass, we can transcend our limitations and leave a lasting impact on the world we call home.

In the years following Maria and Alejandro's passing, their legacy continued to flourish and evolve. The foundation established in their names thrived, carrying on their mission to protect wildlife and preserve cultural heritage.

Under the leadership of a dedicated team, the foundation expanded its reach, establishing partnerships with organizations, governments, and communities worldwide. Their collaborative efforts led to the creation of protected areas, sustainable eco-tourism initiatives, and educational programs that empowered local communities to become guardians of their natural resources.

The foundation also focused on empowering the next generation of conservationists. They provided scholarships, mentorship programs, and research grants to young individuals passionate about environmental stewardship. Through these initiatives, Maria and Alejandro's spirit of love and devotion to the planet continued to inspire and guide future leaders.

Over time, the impact of their work became increasingly evident. The wildlife populations that once faced decline started to rebound, and fragile ecosystems were nurtured back to health. Costa Rica, once again, became a shining example of successful conservation efforts, and its natural beauty flourished.

Meanwhile, Maria and Alejandro's love story remained an enduring symbol of hope and resilience. Their tale continued to be celebrated through art, literature, and even a dedicated museum that showcased their journey and its profound impact on the world.

The museum attracted visitors from far and wide, allowing them to immerse themselves in the incredible story of two individuals who, through their love, had transformed the world around them.

isitors left inspired and filled with a renewed sense of purpose, ready to make their own positive ontributions to the planet.

s the years passed, Maria and Alejandro's names became synonymous with environmental and ultural conservation. They were posthumously honored with numerous awards and recognitions, ementing their place in history as true environmental heroes.

heir love story became a symbol of the power of love, compassion, and resilience in the face of dversity. It served as a reminder that every individual has the potential to make a difference, and that a ngle act of love can ripple outward, creating a wave of positive change that transcends generations.

nd so, the tale of Maria and Alejandro lives on, inspiring countless individuals to cherish the natural orld, protect its inhabitants, and nurture the bonds of love and compassion in their own lives. Their

gacy serves as a beacon of hope, reminding us that even in the face of challenges, love has the power transform the world.

a small coastal town of Costa Rica, nestled between the azure waters of the Pacific Ocean and the ush rainforests, a monument was erected in honor of Maria and Alejandro. The monument stood tall nd proud, overlooking the pristine beaches they had loved so dearly.

ocals and visitors alike would come to the monument, drawn by the enduring love story it epresented. They would sit on the nearby benches, sharing stories and memories of their own

xperiences with love and resilience. The monument became a place of solace, inspiration, and eflection.

n the anniversary of Maria and Alejandro's passing, the town would come alive with a vibrant elebration of their lives and legacy. Festivities would fill the air, featuring music, dance, and heartfelt peeches that honored their remarkable journey.

uring the celebration, a surprise announcement was made. The Maria and Alejandro Foundation evealed a new initiative: a scholarship program specifically designed to support young couples facing nallenges with fertility. The program aimed to provide financial assistance for fertility treatments, motional support, and guidance to those who longed to build a family but faced difficulties in doing ).

he announcement touched the hearts of many, offering hope to those who had experienced similar ruggles. It symbolized Maria and Alejandro's unwavering belief in the power of love and their desire extend their legacy of compassion and support to others.

s the years went by, the scholarship program thrived, helping numerous couples realize their dreams f having children. The recipients would often gather at the monument, sharing their stories of ratitude, joy, and the unexpected surprises that had brought them together as families.

addition to the scholarship program, the Maria and Alejandro Foundation continued to expand its onservation efforts. It partnered with international organizations, governments, and local communities to tackle pressing environmental challenges, ranging from climate change and deforestation to wildlife trafficking.

The foundation's impact grew exponentially, with projects spanning continents and involving countless individuals inspired by Maria and Alejandro's story. Their message of love, resilience, and environmental stewardship resonated globally, igniting a collective consciousness for the urgent need protect and preserve our planet.

In recognition of their outstanding contributions, Maria and Alejandro were posthumously awarded th prestigious Global Environmental Legacy Award. The award ceremony, held in Costa Rica, united world leaders, activists, and scientists, who celebrated their unwavering commitment to the Earth's well-being.

The legacy of Maria and Alejandro continued to inspire future generations. Schools integrated their story into their curriculum, teaching children about the power of love, the importance of conservation, and the remarkable impact that ordinary individuals can have on the world.

As time moved forward, Maria and Alejandro's tale became more than a story—it became a symbol of hope, a reminder that love, in its purest form, has the power to overcome obstacles and create a lasting legacy of change.

And so, the memory of Maria and Alejandro lives on, woven into the fabric of Costa Rica's history and celebrated across the globe. Their story continues to spark conversations, ignite passions, and inspire acts of kindness and compassion in every corner of the world. Their love story is a testament to the

enduring power of love, the beauty of unexpected surprises, and the transformative impact that one couple's love can have on the world.

Years after Maria and Alejandro's passing, an extraordinary event took place in Costa Rica. The town that had embraced their love story became the backdrop for a serendipitous encounter between two individuals—a young couple, Luis and Sofia, who had heard about the legendary tale of Maria and Alejandro.

Luis and Sofia were deeply in love and had been trying to conceive a child for years without success. They had traveled from afar, seeking solace and inspiration in the place that had become synonymous with love, resilience, and the power of unexpected surprises.

While exploring the town, Luis and Sofia stumbled upon the monument dedicated to Maria and Alejandro. As they stood before it, their hands intertwined, a feeling of hope and reassurance washed over them. They believed that their visit would bring them closer to their dream of starting a family.

Little did they know that the universe had a sweet surprise in store for them—one that would forever intertwine their lives with the legacy of Maria and Alejandro. As they turned to leave, a woman approached them, her eyes shimmering with kindness and wisdom.

The woman introduced herself as Rosa, an elder who had known Maria and Alejandro during their time in the town. She had witnessed the growth of their love and their unwavering dedication to making a difference. In her hands, Rosa held a small package wrapped in delicate paper.

With a gentle smile, Rosa presented the package to Luis and Sofia, saying, "Maria and Alejandro's love has brought me to you. In this package, you will find a precious gift—a small wooden box containing a special message."

Eagerly, Luis and Sofia opened the package, revealing the beautifully crafted wooden box within. Inside the box, they found a handwritten letter from Maria and Alejandro, composed years ago, but meant to be delivered to them at this very moment.

The letter spoke of love, resilience, and the power of unexpected surprises. Maria and Alejandro shared their own struggles with infertility and their unwavering belief that love could transcend biological barriers. They encouraged Luis and Sofia never to lose hope, to cherish their love, and to embrace the journey they were on.

Tears of gratitude streamed down Luis and Sofia's faces as they absorbed the profound words of Maria and Alejandro. In that moment, they felt a deep connection to the couple, as if their souls were intertwined across time.

Emboldened by the message, Luis and Sofia returned home, carrying Maria and Alejandro's love with them. They continued to pursue their dream of having a family, supported by the wisdom and hope instilled in them by the remarkable couple.

Months passed, and to their joy and astonishment, Luis and Sofia discovered that they were expecting a child. The sweet surprise they had hoped for had become a reality. Their hearts overflowed with gratitude for the love and guidance that Maria and Alejandro had bestowed upon them.

Their child, born into a world touched by the extraordinary love of Maria and Alejandro, grew up hearing the tale of their connection to the legendary couple. As they grew, the child, named Marcela, embodied the same spirit of compassion, resilience, and love that had characterized Maria and Alejandro's journey.

Marcela, inspired by her parents' story and the legacy of Maria and Alejandro, dedicated her life to continuing their mission of environmental preservation and supporting couples facing fertility challenges. She became a renowned advocate, counselor, and educator, spreading hope and empowering others with her words and actions.

Through Marcela's efforts, the scholarship program established by the Maria and Alejandro Foundation expanded, offering support and guidance to countless couples on their path to parenthood. Her compassion and knowledge touched the lives of many, serving as a living testament to the enduring legacy of love that began with Maria and Alejandro.

And so, the tale of Maria and Alejandro reached new heights, transcending

The tale of Maria and Alejandro continued to inspire generations to come. Their love story became the subject of a best-selling novel that captured the hearts of readers worldwide. The book was adapted into a critically acclaimed film, bringing their extraordinary journey to the big screen once again.

The film touched the hearts of millions, igniting a global movement centered around love, resilience, and the power of unexpected surprises. Viewers were moved to take action in their own lives, embracing the belief that love can conquer all obstacles.

In honor of Maria and Alejandro's profound impact, the Costa Rican government established an annual celebration called "Love and Resilience Day." The day was dedicated to recognizing and honoring individuals and couples who embodied the spirit of love and resilience in their own lives, making a positive difference in their communities and the world.

The Love and Resilience Day festivities included a grand ceremony in which exceptional individuals were awarded the Maria and Alejandro Love and Resilience Medal. This prestigious honor recognized those who had overcome adversity and made significant contributions to society, echoing the values that Maria and Alejandro had embodied.

The legacy of Maria and Alejandro extended beyond their love story and conservation efforts. Their journey also inspired scientists and researchers to delve deeper into the mysteries of fertility. Through their story, new advancements were made in reproductive medicine, offering hope to couples facing similar challenges.

As the years passed, the impact of Maria and Alejandro's love continued to ripple outward. Their foundation expanded its initiatives to address global environmental issues, collaborating with international organizations to protect endangered species, restore ecosystems, and advocate for sustainable practices.

Their story became a staple in Costa Rican culture, passed down through generations as a testament to the enduring power of love and the importance of preserving the natural world. The monument

dedicated to Maria and Alejandro remained a cherished symbol of hope, where visitors from around the world would come to pay their respects and find solace in its presence.

In a testament to the far-reaching impact of their love, a group of young scholars established the Maria and Alejandro Love and Resilience Research Institute. This institute focused on exploring the profound effects of love, resilience, and unexpected surprises on human well-being, relationships, and societal change. Its findings provided valuable insights that influenced fields ranging from psychology to social sciences.

As the world faced new challenges and transitions, Maria and Alejandro's story continued to serve as a beacon of hope. Their unwavering belief in the power of love and their determination to make a difference inspired generations to come together, united by a shared vision of a more compassionate and sustainable world.

And so, the tale of Maria and Alejandro remains etched in the hearts and minds of people around the globe. Their love story continues to inspire individuals to embrace the unexpected, to persevere in the face of adversity, and to cultivate a deep sense of love and compassion for one another and the planet we call home.

In a remote village of Costa Rica, nestled amidst the verdant rainforest, a young girl named Lucia discovered an old, worn-out journal hidden within the hollow of a tree. Intrigued, she opened its pages and found herself immersed in the story of Maria and Alejandro, a tale that had captivated the world for generations.

As Lucia delved deeper into the journal, she realized that it held a secret—a hidden message left behind by Maria and Alejandro themselves. The message spoke of a forgotten treasure, a secret garden concealed within the heart of the rainforest. It was a place where the true magic of their love story had taken root.

Driven by curiosity and a sense of adventure, Lucia embarked on a quest to uncover the hidden garden. With the journal as her guide, she traversed rugged terrain, crossed rivers, and braved the elements, guided by an invisible thread woven by Maria and Alejandro's enduring love.

Finally, Lucia arrived at the heart of the rainforest, where she found a mystical place teeming with vibrant flowers, singing birds, and sparkling waterfalls. The atmosphere hummed with an energy that seemed to transcend the natural world—a testament to the profound love that had bloomed here.

In the center of the garden stood a majestic tree, its branches reaching towards the sky. Lucia approached the tree, her heart pounding with anticipation. As she reached out to touch its bark, a gentle breeze swept through the garden, whispering a melody that resonated deep within her soul.

In that moment, Lucia felt an indescribable connection to Maria and Alejandro, as if their spirits enveloped her. The air shimmered with a soft glow, and a figure materialized before her—the ethereal presence of Maria herself.

Maria's voice, filled with warmth and love, echoed through the garden. She shared her gratitude for Lucia's journey, for carrying their story into the future. Maria revealed that the garden held a special power—the ability to grant the deepest desires of those who entered with a pure heart.

Moved by Lucia's own longing for love and connection, Maria reached out and placed a single seed in Lucia's hand—a seed of pure, unconditional love. She explained that this seed held within it the power to bring people together, to heal wounds, and to nurture the bonds of love.

With gratitude and determination, Lucia accepted the seed, understanding the profound responsibility bestowed upon her. She vowed to carry Maria and Alejandro's legacy forward, nurturing the seed of love and spreading its magic throughout the world.

Lucia returned to her village, her heart ablaze with purpose. She shared her encounter with Maria and Alejandro's hidden garden and the seed of love with the villagers, igniting a collective spark of hope and inspiration. Together, they formed a community dedicated to cultivating love, compassion, and unity, not just within their village, but far beyond its boundaries.

As the seed of love took root and blossomed, the village transformed into a haven of connection and understanding. The villagers embraced one another with open hearts, supporting each other through joys and sorrows, and finding solace in the knowledge that they were part of something greater—a legacy of love that transcended time and place.

News of the village's transformation spread, capturing the attention of people near and far. Visitors flocked to witness the power of love in action, drawn to the village that had become a living testament to Maria and Alejandro's extraordinary journey.

Inspired by Lucia and her community, other villages and towns across Costa Rica and beyond began to cultivate their own seeds of love. The movement spread like wildfire, encompassing cities, countries, and continents. Love became the driving force behind societal change, forging connections, dismantling barriers, and healing wounds that had long divided humanity.

The legacy of Maria and Alejandro's love continued

The legacy of Maria and Alejandro's love continued to ripple across the world, transcending boundaries and inspiring countless individuals to embrace love as a transformative force.

Lucia, now an ambassador of love and connection, traveled from village to village, sharing the story of Maria and Alejandro and the power of the hidden garden. She organized workshops and gatherings where people could come together, exchange stories, and nurture their own seeds of love.

In collaboration with the Maria and Alejandro Foundation, Lucia spearheaded initiatives to promote love and unity on a global scale. They organized international conferences, bringing together thought leaders, activists, and ordinary individuals who were passionate about cultivating a more loving world.

The foundation expanded its scholarship program, offering opportunities for young people to study the interconnectedness of love, compassion, and social change. Graduates of the program became ambassadors of love, working in various fields to create positive, lasting impacts in their communities.

The movement sparked by Maria and Alejandro's love story gained recognition from influential organizations and leaders. Lucia and her team collaborated with the United Nations, dedicating a special day each year to celebrate the power of love and its role in achieving peace and harmony worldwide.

As the years passed, the seeds of love planted by Lucia and her community grew into towering trees of compassion, kindness, and understanding. Communities around the world embraced the principles of love, fostering inclusive societies that valued empathy and connection above all else.

The world witnessed a significant shift in how conflicts were approached. Dialogue and understanding became the foundation for resolving disputes, replacing violence and animosity. Love became the guiding force in political decisions, social policies, and environmental stewardship.

hrough their collective efforts, the legacy of Maria and Alejandro became a beacon of hope for future enerations. The hidden garden in the rainforest, once known only to a few, became a sanctuary open to ll. People from every corner of the globe made pilgrimages to the garden, finding solace, inspiration, nd a renewed sense of purpose.

n the garden, visitors discovered their own seeds of love, each unique and ready to flourish. They arried these seeds back to their communities, nurturing them with care, and creating a network of nterconnected love that spanned continents.

Vith each act of kindness, every embrace, and every expression of love, the world was transformed. ove became the common language, dissolving the barriers of language, culture, and ideology. People ealized that love was not limited to romantic relationships but could be the foundation of all human nteractions.

nd so, the story of Maria and Alejandro, sparked by their unexpected love and sweet surprises, ecame a catalyst for a global revolution of love. Their legacy lives on in the hearts of those who carry heir story, nurturing seeds of love and cultivating a world where compassion and connection are the uiding principles of humanity.

ucia, the young girl who discovered the journal and embarked on the quest, lived in a small village in 1e heart of Costa Rica. The village was nestled amidst the lush greenery of the country's vibrant ainforest. Surrounded by breathtaking natural beauty, Lucia grew up in a community that valued the armonious relationship between humans and nature. The village was a close-knit community where veryone knew each other, fostering a strong sense of connection and belonging.

ulia's children, Maria, Anna, and Frank, played an integral role in the unfolding story. Let's explore heir involvement:

Iaria, the eldest of Julia's children, grew up hearing stories about the hidden garden from her mother. ntrigued by the tales, she developed a deep fascination for the enchanting place. As she became older,

Iaria carried on her mother's legacy, visiting the garden herself and discovering the profound love that manated from its every corner.

nspired by her mother's journey and driven by her own connection to the hidden garden, Maria edicated her life to the preservation of the rainforest and its remarkable biodiversity. She became an nvironmental activist, working tirelessly to raise awareness about the importance of conservation and ustainable practices.

nna, Julia's middle child, possessed a natural affinity for art and creativity. She inherited her mother's rtistic spirit and found solace and inspiration in the hidden garden. As she grew older, Anna expressed er love for the garden through her artwork, creating vibrant paintings and sculptures that captured the ssence of its beauty.

nna's artwork became renowned globally, drawing attention to the delicate balance between humanity nd nature. Her pieces served as a reminder of the interconnectedness of all living beings and the need to protect and cherish the natural world. Anna's creations became a catalyst for environmental conversations and raised funds for conservation efforts.

Frank, the youngest of Julia's children, inherited his mother's sense of adventure and curiosity. He developed a deep passion for exploration and dedicated his life to studying the rainforest's rich ecosystems and indigenous cultures. Frank became an anthropologist, working closely with local communities to document their traditional knowledge and promote cultural preservation.

Through his work, Frank shed light on the importance of indigenous wisdom and their harmonious relationship with the rainforest. He advocated for their rights and the protection of their lands, emphasizing the vital role they play in preserving the biodiversity and cultural heritage of Costa Rica

Maria, Anna, and Frank, each driven by their unique passions and influenced by their mother's connection to the hidden garden, collaborated on various projects. They organized art exhibitions, environmental initiatives, and cultural events that celebrated the intertwined beauty of nature, art, and indigenous wisdom.

Their collective efforts had a profound impact on their local community and beyond. Through their work, they fostered a deep appreciation for the natural world, inspired creativity, and promoted the importance of sustainable living. They also encouraged dialogue and understanding among different cultures, bridging divides and fostering a sense of unity and love.

The love and connection that Julia's children shared with the hidden garden and their commitment to preserving its magic helped create a lasting legacy. Their actions touched the lives of countless individuals, igniting a passion for environmental stewardship, artistic expression, and cultural preservation.

As Maria, Anna, and Frank carried forward their mother's love for the hidden garden, their individual journeys intertwined with the greater narrative of love, nature, and human connection. Together, they became champions of the rainforest and advocates for a more compassionate and sustainable world.

Anna, being a lesbian during a time when society was less accepting, faced additional obstacles on her personal journey. While her love for the hidden garden and her artistic endeavors remained central to

her life, she also had to navigate the complexities of her sexual orientation within a society that might not have fully embraced her identity.

1. Personal Acceptance and Growth: Anna's journey began with self-discovery and self-acceptance. She had to overcome internal struggles and societal pressures to embrace her true identity as a lesbian. Over time, Anna found the strength and courage to celebrate her authentic self and live her life with pride and integrity.

2. Artistic Expression and LGBTQ+ Advocacy: Anna's artistic expression became an even more powerful medium for advocating LGBTQ+ rights and promoting acceptance. Through her artwork, she conveyed the beauty, love, and diversity of same-sex relationships, challenging societal norms and inspiring others to embrace inclusivity and compassion.

3. Creating Safe Spaces: Understanding the importance of safe spaces, Anna actively worked to create supportive environments where LGBTQ+ individuals could freely express themselves. She organized art exhibitions, workshops, and events that showcased the work of LGBTQ+ artists and provided platforms for open discussions and dialogue. These spaces served as catalysts for fostering understanding, empathy, and acceptance.

4. LGBTQ+ Activism and Community Support: Anna became a prominent voice in the local LGBTQ+ community, advocating for equality, acceptance, and the protection of LGBTQ+ rights. She collaborated with LGBTQ+ organizations, participated in Pride events, and engaged in grassroots activism. Anna's contributions helped build bridges between the LGBTQ+ community and society at large, fostering greater understanding and acceptance.

5. Family Acceptance and Support: Anna's journey also involved navigating her relationships with her family members. While there may have been initial challenges and misunderstandings, her love for her family and their shared history eventually fostered understanding and acceptance. With time, Anna's family came to embrace her fully, providing the support and love she needed to thrive.

6. Empowering LGBTQ+ Youth: Recognizing the importance of empowering LGBTQ+ youth, Anna became a mentor and role model for young individuals who were navigating their own journeys of self-discovery. She used her experiences to provide guidance, support, and a sense of belonging to those who might be facing similar challenges. Anna's presence in the LGBTQ+ community became a source of inspiration and hope for others seeking acceptance and love.

7. Cultural Transformation: Anna's activism, advocacy, and artistic contributions played a part in challenging societal attitudes and fostering cultural transformation. Her openness and authenticity contributed to shifting perspectives, promoting dialogue, and cultivating a more inclusive and accepting society. Through her actions, she helped create a world where individuals of all sexual orientations could be embraced and celebrated for who they are.

Anna's journey as a lesbian within the context of a less accepting society brought forth unique challenges, but also provided her with an opportunity to be a catalyst for change. Her love for the hidden garden, her artistic expression, and her LGBTQ+ advocacy all converged to make a profound

impact on both the artistic and LGBTQ+ communities, fostering a more inclusive and compassionate society for future generations

Maria's experience of being in space would have undoubtedly shaped her perspective on life and her connection to the hidden garden. Here's an updated glimpse into Maria's life, considering her journey as an astronaut:

1. The Cosmic Perspective: Maria's journey to space opened her eyes to the vastness and beauty of the universe. From the unique vantage point of the cosmos, she witnessed the Earth as a fragile, interconnected ecosystem. Maria's experiences instilled in her a deep sense of awe and

reverence for the natural world, strengthening her commitment to environmental conservation and the protection of the hidden garden.

2. Sharing the Wonders: Maria's time in space ignited a passion for sharing her experiences with others. She became an enthusiastic advocate for space exploration and a captivating storyteller, recounting her observations of the Earth, the stars, and the wonders of the universe. Through speaking engagements, educational programs, and media appearances, Maria inspired others to appreciate the beauty and interconnectedness of all life on Earth.

3. Bridge between Space and Nature: Maria found a profound connection between her experiences in space and her love for the hidden garden. She drew parallels between the delicate ecosystems of the rainforest and the delicate balance of life on Earth. Maria's unique perspective fostered a deeper understanding of the importance of sustainable practices and the need to preserve Earth's natural resources.

4. Collaborations with Scientists and Artists: Maria collaborated with scientists, artists, and researchers to bridge the realms of space exploration, environmental science, and artistic expression. Through interdisciplinary projects, they sought to explore the intersections between science, art, and the hidden garden. Maria's firsthand experiences of the cosmos provided inspiration for artists, fueling their creative expression and deepening their connection to nature.

5. Environmental Activism on a Global Scale: Maria's space journey propelled her environmental activism to a global level. She leveraged her platform as an astronaut to advocate for sustainable practices, raise awareness about climate change, and emphasize the interconnectedness of all living beings. Maria's unique perspective and experiences resonated with people around the world, inspiring them to take action to protect the planet.

6. Research and Exploration: Maria remained involved in scientific research and exploration, collaborating with space agencies and environmental organizations. Her experiences in space influenced her focus on studying Earth's ecosystems, climate patterns, and the impact of human activities on the environment. Through her research efforts, Maria contributed to the understanding of our planet and its delicate balance.

7. Legacy of Exploration and Love: Maria's journey as an astronaut and her love for the hidden garden became intertwined in her legacy. She dedicated her life to fostering a deeper connection between humanity and the natural world, inspiring future generations to explore,

appreciate, and protect both the mysteries of outer space and the treasures found within the hidden garden.

Maria's experiences in space enriched her understanding of the fragility and interconnectedness of life on Earth. Her passion for sharing her cosmic perspective and her commitment to environmental conservation resonated with people worldwide, creating a ripple effect of love and appreciation for the beauty of our planet. Her legacy as an astronaut and advocate for the hidden garden continues to inspire and shape the way we view our place in the universe.

In an unexpected twist, Anna's journey led her to find love in the most unlikely of places—the near planet Orxi. Here's a glimpse into this fascinating development in Anna's life:

While pursuing her passion for exploration and cultural preservation, Anna embarked on a scientific expedition to study the biodiversity and indigenous cultures of Costa Rica. During her research, she encountered a mysterious artifact that hinted at a connection between the hidden garden and a distant planet called Orxi.

Intrigued by the possibility of an interplanetary relationship, Anna's curiosity led her to delve deeper into the subject. She discovered that Orxi was a planet known for its advanced civilization, rich cultural traditions, and remarkable biodiversity. It was a world where love and acceptance were embraced, regardless of gender or sexual orientation.

Driven by her thirst for knowledge and an open heart, Anna embarked on an interstellar journey to Orxi. There, she encountered a vibrant and inclusive society, where different forms of love were celebrated and respected. It was on Orxi that Anna met a fellow adventurer named Rhea—a compassionate and free-spirited individual who shared Anna's love for exploration, art, and the preservation of cultural heritage.

As Anna and Rhea spent time together, their connection grew deeper, transcending the boundaries of space and time. They embarked on joint expeditions, exploring the diverse landscapes of Orxi, documenting its cultural traditions, and fostering understanding between their two worlds. Their love flourished amidst the wonders of a planet where acceptance and inclusivity were cherished values.

Anna's newfound love on Orxi became an emblem of the power of love to transcend boundaries, whether they be societal norms or interplanetary distances. Their relationship symbolized the beauty of diversity and the importance of embracing love in all its forms.

Returning to Earth, Anna and Rhea carried their love with them, becoming advocates for acceptance and understanding between different cultures and societies. They shared their extraordinary journey and the lessons they learned about love, diversity, and inclusivity. Their story became an inspiration, reminding people of the boundless possibilities that love can bring, even across the vastness of space.

Anna's love story with Rhea on the near planet Orxi became a testament to the power of connection, resilience, and the willingness to explore beyond the familiar. It challenged societal norms and showcased the beauty of love's universal language, reminding humanity of the importance of acceptance, understanding, and celebrating love in all its forms.

Rhea, the person Anna found love with on the planet Orxi, was 28 years old and possessed a remarkable talent for languages. Meanwhile, Anna embarked on a journey of language learning, gradually acquiring new linguistic skills over time. Here's how their unique dynamics unfolded:

When Anna first arrived on Orxi, she found herself immersed in a vibrant and diverse society with a multitude of languages spoken. Fascinated by the linguistic richness, Anna was eager to communicate and connect with the people of Orxi. It was during this time that she encountered Rhea, a gifted linguist who spoke multiple languages fluently.

Rhea, at the age of 28, possessed an innate talent for acquiring languages effortlessly. They had dedicated years to studying and mastering various tongues spoken on Orxi, enabling them to bridge cultural gaps and foster understanding among different communities.

Inspired by Rhea's linguistic prowess, Anna was drawn to their passion for communication and the power of language. Recognizing the importance of connecting with others, Anna expressed her desire to learn the languages of Orxi, albeit starting with basic phrases and expressions.

Impressed by Anna's enthusiasm and commitment, Rhea gladly took on the role of Anna's language mentor. Together, they embarked on a journey of language learning, with Rhea patiently teaching Anna the intricacies of each tongue spoken on Orxi. They practiced conversational skills, delved into cultural nuances, and embraced the beauty of shared language as a means to foster deeper connections.

As time passed, Anna gradually became conversational in the languages of Orxi, thanks to Rhea's guidance and her own dedication. Although not as fluent as Rhea, Anna's growing linguistic abilities allowed her to engage with the people of Orxi more intimately. Through language, she developed a profound appreciation for their cultural heritage and forged deeper connections with the local communities.

The language-learning dynamic between Anna and Rhea became a cornerstone of their relationship. They celebrated the power of communication, the beauty of shared languages, and the ability to bridge cultural gaps through understanding and empathy. Their journey exemplified the transformative power of language in fostering connection and promoting inclusivity.

Together, Anna and Rhea continued to explore the wonders of Orxi, championing intercultural exchange and celebrating the diversity of languages and traditions they encountered. Their unique dynamic, with Rhea's linguistic expertise and Anna's growing language skills, became a testament to the importance of open-mindedness, the willingness to learn, and the power of communication in building meaningful relationships.

In the end, their shared love for language and the joy of connecting with others helped strengthen their bond, allowing their relationship to flourish amidst the tapestry of linguistic diversity on the planet Orxi

The language spoken on the planet Orxi, called Orxian, presented a unique challenge to Anna due to its complexity and harsh characteristics. However, driven by her determination and love for Rhea, Anna embarked on an intensive language learning journey. Here's how their story unfolds:

Their journey highlighted the power of language as a tool for understanding, acceptance, and unity. Anna's ability to speak Orxian not only enriched her relationship with Rhea but also fostered a deeper sense of belonging and integration within the Orxian community.

In the end, Anna's dedication and hard work in learning Orxian showcased the transformative power of love and language, bridging gaps and embracing diversity. It became a testament to the strength of their relationship and their unwavering commitment to understanding and celebrating one another.

One fateful day, Anna and Rhea had the opportunity to meet Rorp, a respected village leader on the planet Orxi. Little did they know that Rorp held a deep secret, one that would reveal a hidden aspect of Orxi's history and significantly impact their understanding of the planet. Here's how their encounter unfolded:

Rorp, known for his wisdom and esteemed position within the Orxian community, invited Anna and Rhea to his humble abode. As they sat around a crackling fire, Rorp spoke of Orxi's ancient past, unveiling a secret that had been kept hidden for generations.

With a hushed voice, Rorp revealed that Orxi was not merely a planet of natural wonders and cultural diversity—it also harbored a mystical connection to the stars. He explained that the people of Orxi possessed an ancient knowledge of celestial energies, passed down through the ages.

In a moment of revelation, Rorp shared that Orxi had once been home to an ancient civilization that had mastered interstellar travel. They were explorers who ventured far beyond their home planet, visiting distant galaxies and exchanging knowledge with extraterrestrial beings.

However, as time passed, the Orxian civilization faced a great calamity. Their advanced technology failed, leading to the collapse of their interstellar capabilities. In order to protect the planet's remaining resources, they chose to retreat into isolation, ensuring the preservation of Orxi's natural wonders and safeguarding their cultural heritage.

Anna and Rhea listened with wide-eyed wonder, realizing that Orxi's mystique extended far beyond what they had previously known. The revelation deepened their appreciation for the planet's rich history and its people's resilience.

Inspired by Rorp's revelation, Anna, Rhea, and Rorp formed an unexpected alliance. Together, they embarked on a mission to uncover more about Orxi's interstellar legacy, delving into ancient texts, studying artifacts, and seeking wisdom from the oldest inhabitants of the planet.

Their joint efforts led them to discover hidden ruins, ancient star maps, and tales passed down through generations. They pieced together the fragments of Orxi's interstellar history, connecting the dots between the planet's ancient civilization and its current state.

As their research progressed, Anna, Rhea, and Rorp began to understand that Orxi's isolation was not only about protecting its resources but also about preserving a delicate balance between the natural world and the cosmic energies that permeated the planet.

Their findings revealed that the hidden garden, the vibrant rainforest that had first captivated Anna's heart, held a deeper significance. It was a sanctuary of life intertwined with the celestial forces that flowed through Orxi, a unique and harmonious blend of terrestrial and cosmic energies.

Armed with this newfound knowledge, Anna, Rhea, and Rorp shared their discoveries with the Orxian community. The revelation ignited a renewed sense of wonder, reminding the inhabitants of their connection to the stars and inspiring them to embrace their interstellar legacy.

From that day forward, Orxi embraced its identity as a planet intricately linked to the cosmos. The people of Orxi celebrated their interstellar heritage, acknowledging the beauty of their natural world a a reflection of the greater cosmic tapestry.

Anna, Rhea, and Rorp became revered figures, known for their role in unraveling Orxi's hidden secret They continued to explore, research, and foster understanding between Orxi and other civilizations, sharing the wisdom they gained along the way.

The encounter with Rorp and the revelation of Orxi's interstellar past enriched Anna and Rhea's love story, deepening their connection to the planet and to each other. They embarked on a lifelong missior to protect Orxi's delicate balance and to ensure that its interstellar legacy would be preserved for futur

Intrigued by Rorp's revelation about Orxi's interstellar past, Anna and Rhea leaned in closer, eager to hear the story of Rorp's own journey to the end of space. Rorp, with a glint of nostalgia in his eyes, began to recount his extraordinary tale:

Many years ago, Rorp had been a young and curious explorer. Driven by an insatiable thirst for knowledge, he embarked on a daring mission to unravel the mysteries of the universe. Equipped with small spacecraft crafted by Orxi's ancient civilization, Rorp ventured beyond the boundaries of their star system, embarking on a journey that would forever change his perception of the cosmos.

As he traveled deeper into the unknown, Rorp encountered breathtaking celestial phenomena— nebulae that danced with vibrant colors, distant galaxies that sparkled like diamonds in the vast expanse, and cosmic forces that defied comprehension. Every moment of his interstellar voyage filled him with awe and wonder, expanding his understanding of the universe.

During his travels, Rorp had the privilege of encountering civilizations from distant galaxies, each wit their own unique customs, technologies, and wisdom. He engaged in exchanges of knowledge, witnessing the diversity and interconnectedness of life across the cosmos.

One particularly profound encounter shaped Rorp's perspective forever. He encountered an advanced civilization whose members possessed an extraordinary ability to tap into the energy of the stars. They had harnessed the cosmic forces to create sustainable technologies, heal the wounded, and even influence the growth of celestial bodies.

Inspired by their harmonious coexistence with the cosmos, Rorp dedicated himself to understanding th intricate balance between Orxi's terrestrial wonders and the cosmic energies that flowed through it. He realized that the ancient Orxian civilization had once achieved a similar harmony, and it was their desire to protect this balance that led to their retreat into isolation.

Rorp's own journey through the cosmos allowed him to glimpse the magnificence and interconnectedness of the universe. He returned to Orxi with a profound sense of responsibility—to protect the planet's delicate equilibrium and share the knowledge he had gained with his fellow Orxians.

As Rorp finished his tale, Anna and Rhea were filled with a renewed sense of awe and purpose. Rorp's journey validated their own discoveries and deepened their commitment to preserve Orxi's interstellar legacy.

Together, Anna, Rhea, and Rorp forged an unbreakable bond, united by their shared love for Orxi and their determination to honor its interstellar heritage. They became advocates for the protection of the natural world, the celebration of cosmic interconnectedness, and the fostering of harmony between civilizations.

Their story spread far and wide, captivating the hearts and minds of individuals from different corners of the universe. The tale of Anna, Rhea, and Rorp served as a reminder of the boundless wonders that awaited those who dared to explore, the wisdom that could be gained from interstellar connections, and the importance of preserving the delicate balance between worlds.

From that day forward, Orxi became known not only for its natural beauty but also for its deep cosmic connection—a testament to the resilience of its people and their commitment to embracing all things.

Maria and Frank, moved to Europe and lived every day as happy as they could be.
Anna and Rhea, stayed together and continue to travel all over the universe.
The point to the story is that we must respect what lives throughs at you and is never to late to learn.

# The Jungle

Once upon a time, in a remote and uncharted corner of the world, there lay a lush and mysterious jungle island. Hidden amidst its dense foliage were two unlikely companions, Amelia and Gabriel, who found themselves stranded there after a disastrous shipwreck.

Amelia, a resourceful young woman in her early twenties, and Gabriel, a seasoned adventurer in his late thirties, had managed to survive all these years on the island by forging a unique bond and learning to adapt to the wild environment. Over time, their isolation turned into a peculiar camaraderie, as they shared their stories, fears, and dreams for the future.

At first, they clung to the hope that someone would come to their rescue, but as months turned into years, that glimmer of hope began to fade. No ships passed by, and no planes flew overhead. They resigned themselves to the fact that they were forgotten, lost in a world of their own.

Despite the absence of civilization, Amelia and Gabriel embraced their surroundings and grew to appreciate the beauty and dangers of the island. Amelia's knowledge of botany helped them identify edible plants and find fresh water sources. Gabriel, with his survival skills, became adept at constructing shelters and crafting tools from the island's natural resources. Together, they built a small but secure refuge where they felt safe from the island's unpredictable elements.

As the years went by, their friendship blossomed into something deeper. The shared struggles and moments of joy brought them closer, and a strong bond formed between them. However, deep down, they yearned for the familiar comforts of home and to share their lives with their loved ones once again.

One day, while exploring a remote corner of the island, they stumbled upon an ancient stone tablet. Etched into its weathered surface were markings that, upon closer inspection, revealed a map. Excitement and trepidation surged through their veins as they realized it could hold the key to their long-awaited escape.

Using their combined skills and knowledge, they deciphered the map's symbols, leading them to believe that a hidden cave held the answers they sought. Days turned into weeks as they carefully navigated treacherous terrain, overcoming obstacles and enduring the jungle's unforgiving trials.

Finally, after a grueling trek, they discovered the secret cave. As they entered its depths, a beam of sunlight pierced through a crack in the ceiling, illuminating an ancient altar. On it rested a golden artifact—a long-forgotten communication device.

Amelia and Gabriel's hearts swelled with hope. With trembling hands, they managed to power on the device. Miraculously, a weak signal emerged, reaching far beyond the island. They were overcome with joy as they heard the crackle of a distant voice—a voice belonging to a search and rescue team.

With the help of their newfound communication, they relayed their exact location, desperate to finally leave the island they had called home for the past 23 years. The rescue team was astounded, as they had believed no survivors remained from the ill-fated shipwreck so long ago.

After a few days of anticipation and careful planning, a helicopter finally descended upon the island, its blades beating against the warm tropical air. Tears of relief streamed down Amelia and Gabriel's faces as they bid farewell to the island that had sheltered them for more than two decades.

As the helicopter whisked them away, they held hands, knowing that their unique bond, forged in the wilderness, would never be forgotten. They were returning to a world that had changed immeasurably, but their love for each other and the strength they had gained in their time on the island would forever remain in their hearts

Amelia and Gabriel's return to civilization was a mix of excitement, wonder, and adjustment. The bustling city they encountered overwhelmed their senses after spending so many years in the serene

and untouched wilderness. As they stepped foot into the modern world, they were met with a whirlwind of technology, new customs, and faces they didn't recognize.

News of their remarkable survival spread like wildfire, captivating the public's attention. People marveled at their resilience and endurance, considering their incredible story a testament to the indomitable spirit of humanity. Reporters sought interviews, and their journey became the subject of books and documentaries.

However, amidst the newfound fame, Amelia and Gabriel longed for a sense of normalcy. They craved the embrace of their families, the warmth of familiar voices, and the simple joys of everyday life. Reconnecting with their loved ones proved to be an emotional and transformative experience, as they shared the tales of their extraordinary adventure, both the trials and the profound moments of growth.

Although their return brought joy and relief, it also presented challenges. Amelia and Gabriel had been absent for over two decades, missing out on the rapid progress and changes in the world. They found themselves catching up on technological advancements, societal shifts, and cultural phenomena that had become woven into the fabric of everyday life.

While they had acclimated to the harsh realities of the jungle island, adapting to the intricacies of contemporary society proved to be an entirely different endeavor. They attended counseling sessions to help them process their transition, seeking guidance in navigating the complexities of a world that had moved on without them.

As the years passed, Amelia and Gabriel channeled their experiences into advocacy work, raising awareness about environmental conservation and the importance of preserving untouched landscapes. Their firsthand encounters with the beauty and fragility of nature became a driving force in their lives, and they dedicated themselves to protecting the natural wonders they had witnessed during their time on the island.

Despite the challenges they faced, Amelia and Gabriel's bond remained unbreakable. Their love had withstood the test of time and the challenges of their extraordinary journey. They chose to embrace the

second chance life had given them, cherishing each moment together and supporting one another through the highs and lows of their ongoing adventure.

Whether it was embarking on new expeditions to remote corners of the world or simply enjoying the tranquility of a sunset on the beach, Amelia and Gabriel found solace and happiness in the simple joys of life. Their remarkable story became a testament to the power of resilience, the endurance of the human spirit, and the unbreakable bonds that can form in the most unexpected of circumstances.

In the years that followed, Amelia and Gabriel continued their explorations, embarking on new adventures across the globe. Their unique perspective and deep appreciation for nature resonated with people from all walks of life, inspiring others to reconnect with the natural world and protect its delicate balance.

They established a foundation dedicated to environmental conservation, using their platform to raise funds, support research, and initiate projects aimed at preserving endangered ecosystems. Their passion

and determination fueled a movement that spread far and wide, garnering support from individuals, organizations, and governments alike.

Amelia became an advocate for sustainable living, promoting eco-friendly practices and urging communities to embrace renewable energy sources. Her expertise in botany and her profound understanding of the interconnectivity of ecosystems made her a sought-after speaker and consultant.

Gabriel, on the other hand, used his survival skills and knowledge gained from their time on the island to train and educate others in wilderness survival and sustainable outdoor practices. He led expeditions and guided aspiring adventurers, instilling in them a deep respect for nature and the importance of leaving no trace.

As their foundation thrived and their influence grew, Amelia and Gabriel's efforts caught the attention of international organizations focused on environmental preservation. They were invited to speak at conferences, collaborate on conservation projects, and contribute to policy discussions, becoming influential voices in shaping a sustainable future.

However, amid their global commitments and environmental endeavors, Amelia and Gabriel never lost sight of their personal journey. They remained deeply connected, their love having weathered the test of time and the challenges that life had thrown their way. They continued to prioritize their relationship, nurturing it with love, understanding, and shared adventures.

Amelia and Gabriel also made it a point to return to the island that had been their home for so many years. It had become a symbol of their resilience and the profound transformation they had undergone. They established a conservation outpost on the island, ensuring its protection and fostering scientific research to better understand its unique ecosystem.

s they grew older, Amelia and Gabriel passed on their knowledge and passion to younger generations, entoring individuals who shared their vision for a sustainable world. Their legacy lived on through e countless lives they had touched, and their story served as a reminder that every individual has the ower to make a difference.

hen the time came for them to depart this world, Amelia and Gabriel did so knowing they had left ehind a lasting impact. Their love, their dedication to the environment, and their unwavering spirit spired generations to come. Their names became synonymous with resilience, adventure, and the rofound connection between humanity and the natural world.

nd so, their story lives on—a testament to the human spirit, the power of love, and the boundless ossibilities that lie within each of us

 the years that followed, the legacy of Amelia and Gabriel continued to flourish, inspiring countless dividuals to embark on their own journeys of self-discovery and environmental stewardship. Their ory became the subject of books, movies, and even a popular documentary series that chronicled their markable tale of survival and resilience.

he foundation they had established expanded its reach, partnering with other organizations and overnments to implement sustainable practices and protect fragile ecosystems around the world.

hrough their advocacy and fundraising efforts, they were able to preserve vast stretches of land, stablish marine sanctuaries, and support scientific research aimed at understanding and mitigating the npacts of climate change.

s their work gained recognition, Amelia and Gabriel received numerous accolades and awards for eir contributions to environmental conservation. Their humility and genuine passion for the cause ndeared them to people from all walks of life. They became ambassadors for global initiatives, using eir influence to champion policies that promoted environmental sustainability and fostered a greater ense of interconnectedness among nations.

espite their busy schedules, Amelia and Gabriel always made time for personal reflection and olitude. They would occasionally retreat to the island where their journey began, finding solace in its ntouched beauty and the memories it held. They would spend days exploring its depths, marveling at e resilience of nature and reminding themselves of the transformative power of their own xperiences.

s the years passed, the world gradually transitioned towards a more sustainable future, thanks in part  the tireless efforts of Amelia, Gabriel, and the countless individuals they had inspired. Renewable nergy sources became the norm, plastic waste was dramatically reduced, and conservation efforts ained widespread support. The planet began to heal, and a newfound harmony between humanity and ature emerged.

melia and Gabriel's love for each other remained steadfast throughout their lives. They celebrated eir golden anniversary surrounded by family, friends, and those who had been touched by their journey. Their love had become a symbol of resilience and the power of human connection, inspiring countless couples to weather the storms of life together and find strength in unity.

In their twilight years, Amelia and Gabriel passed away peacefully, knowing they had left an indelible mark on the world. Their names became synonymous with the transformative power of love, the pursuit of knowledge, and the preservation of our planet.

Their foundation continued to thrive, guided by the principles and values Amelia and Gabriel had instilled. It became a living testament to their enduring legacy, ensuring that their vision for a sustainable and interconnected world would carry on for generations to come.

And so, as the sun set on their extraordinary lives, the world remained eternally grateful for the two individuals who had spent 23 years lost on an isolated island, only to return and change the course of history. Their story serves as a reminder that even in the face of adversity, hope, love, and determination can ignite a spark that transcends time, inspiring us to protect and cherish the planet we call home.

As time went on, the world continued to evolve, shaped by the legacy of Amelia and Gabriel. Their story became ingrained in popular culture, inspiring generations to embrace adventure, appreciate the natural world, and work towards a sustainable future. Their names lived on in books, museums, and even a dedicated day of celebration in their honor.

The foundation they had established flourished, expanding its reach and impact. It became a global force, collaborating with governments, businesses, and communities to implement sustainable practices on a large scale. The foundation's initiatives ranged from reforestation projects and wildlife conservation efforts to advocating for renewable energy and promoting sustainable agriculture.

New technologies emerged, spurred by the need for innovative solutions to environmental challenges. Clean energy became the dominant source of power worldwide, and breakthroughs in recycling and waste management drastically reduced humanity's ecological footprint. The world's oceans, once threatened by pollution and overfishing, began to heal under the care of marine sanctuaries and international conservation agreements.

Amelia and Gabriel's story remained a symbol of hope and resilience, their names synonymous with bravery and determination. Their journey inspired countless explorers, scientists, and conservationists who followed in their footsteps, determined to protect the planet and honor their memory.

Their families, too, carried their legacy forward, establishing scholarships and grants in their names to support education, research, and projects dedicated to environmental preservation. These initiatives nurtured a new generation of leaders who carried the torch of Amelia and Gabriel's vision, ensuring their passion for the planet would endure for years to come.

In the quiet moments of reflection, people would gaze at the stars and remember the couple who had spent 23 years stranded on an island, their resilience and love guiding them through the trials of isolation. Their story continued to inspire, reminding humanity of the strength that lies within each individual and the transformative power of connection.

And so, as time stretched forward, the impact of Amelia and Gabriel's journey rippled through the tapestry of history. The world, forever changed by their presence, thrived in harmony with nature, embracing a sustainable path towards a brighter future. Their remarkable story stands as a testament to the enduring power of the human spirit and the profound impact that two individuals can have on the world.

In the years that followed, a series of remarkable events unfolded, revealing an astonishing twist to Amelia and Gabriel's story. It turned out that during their time on the island, a group of researchers had inadvertently discovered evidence of their presence.

One day, a young scientist named Dr. Emily Collins stumbled upon an old journal buried within the archives of a remote research facility. The journal chronicled the expedition that had gone awry, detailing the shipwreck and the survival of two individuals on the mysterious jungle island. Driven by curiosity, Dr. Collins embarked on a personal mission to uncover the truth.

Through tireless investigation and meticulous research, Dr. Collins managed to piece together the puzzle. She connected the dots between the long-lost shipwreck and the incredible survival story of Amelia and Gabriel. The revelation shook the world, as people marveled at the resilience and endurance of the two individuals who had remained hidden for 23 years.

News of the discovery spread like wildfire, capturing global attention and igniting a renewed fascination with the island. Scientists, explorers, and tourists flocked to the once-forgotten jungle, eager to witness the place that had sheltered Amelia and Gabriel for so long.

As interest grew, a decision was made to transform the island into a protected national park, preserving its unique biodiversity and ensuring its cultural significance would endure. The park became a sanctuary for rare species, a living laboratory for scientists, and a place of solace and reflection for visitors seeking to connect with nature.

Amelia and Gabriel, who had since passed away, were posthumously honored for their extraordinary journey and their role in bringing attention to the island's importance. Monuments were erected in their memory, and their names became forever associated with the island's rich history.

The island's newfound fame and ecological significance propelled it onto the world stage. It became a center for sustainable tourism, with visitors flocking from far and wide to experience its untouched beauty while adhering to strict conservation guidelines. The local communities thrived, benefitting from the opportunities that responsible tourism brought while safeguarding their cultural heritage.

In tribute to Amelia and Gabriel's enduring love, a symbolic annual ceremony was established on the island. Every year, on the anniversary of their rescue, couples from around the world gathered to renew their vows and celebrate the power of love against all odds. It became a joyous occasion, uniting people in their shared appreciation for the resilience of the human spirit.

Amelia and Gabriel's story continued to inspire generations, even after their names became distant echoes of the past. Their tale transcended time, reminding humanity of the inherent strength, courage, and capacity for growth that lies within each individual.

And so, as the years turned into centuries, the island remained a testament to their journey, a beacon of hope and inspiration for all who encountered it. Their legacy, intertwined with the island's history, served as a reminder of the transformative power of love, the beauty of the natural world, and the enduring impact that a single act of resilience can have on the course of human history.

As the centuries passed, the island that had once sheltered Amelia and Gabriel continued to thrive as a symbol of resilience and natural beauty. The national park dedicated to their memory became a model for sustainable conservation efforts worldwide.

In the wake of their story, a global movement for environmental preservation and sustainable living gained momentum. People began to realize the urgent need to protect and restore the Earth's ecosystems, and governments collaborated to implement far-reaching policies to combat climate change and promote conservation.

The descendants of Amelia and Gabriel played an active role in continuing their ancestors' mission. They dedicated themselves to environmental activism, carrying forward the torch of their family's legacy. Inspired by their forebears, they established organizations, led campaigns, and worked tirelessly to ensure the planet's long-term well-being.

Technology also advanced rapidly, offering new solutions to environmental challenges. Clean energy sources became the predominant form of power worldwide, and innovative approaches to waste management and resource utilization drastically reduced humanity's impact on the environment.

Over time, the world experienced a remarkable transformation. The effects of climate change began to reverse as carbon emissions decreased and natural habitats were restored. Biodiversity flourished, and endangered species once on the brink of extinction staged remarkable recoveries. People around the globe began to live in harmony with nature, embracing sustainable practices in all aspects of their lives.

The island that had been Amelia and Gabriel's refuge continued to hold a special place in the hearts of people everywhere. It became a pilgrimage site for those seeking inspiration and solace, a reminder of the resilience of the human spirit and the power of love in the face of adversity.

Every year, on the anniversary of their rescue, a grand celebration took place on the island. The event brought together people from all corners of the world, united in their commitment to environmental stewardship and celebrating the extraordinary legacy of Amelia and Gabriel. It served as a reminder of the profound impact that two individuals, lost and forgotten for 23 years, had on the course of human history.

The island itself remained a pristine oasis, untouched by human development. It continued to be a sanctuary for diverse flora and fauna, providing a safe haven for species on the brink of extinction. Researchers and scientists from around the world flocked to the island, studying its unique ecosystems and drawing inspiration from its undisturbed beauty.

As the world looked back on the story of Amelia and Gabriel, they served as a reminder that the actions of individuals, driven by love, resilience, and a deep connection to the natural world, can shape the course of history. Their legacy inspired future generations to embrace the responsibility of caring for the Earth and preserving its wonders for all who would come after them.

And so, as time moved ever forward, the tale of Amelia and Gabriel remained a cherished legend, etched into the collective memory of humanity. Their story served as a guiding light, illuminating the

path towards a sustainable future where the planet and its inhabitants thrived in harmony, forever grateful for the remarkable journey of two people lost in time.

In the distant future, when the Earth had become a thriving hub of interconnected civilizations, the island that once sheltered Amelia and Gabriel took on a mythical status. The story of their survival and eventual return resonated with generations, serving as a timeless reminder of human resilience, love, and the intrinsic bond between humanity and the natural world.

Explorers and historians dedicated themselves to uncovering the island's secrets, delving deep into its mysteries. Advanced technologies allowed them to map its hidden landscapes and decode its ancient past. They discovered that the island possessed a unique energy, a source of harmony and rejuvenation that radiated throughout its surroundings.

Recognizing the island's immense potential, the United World Council—an international governing body formed to address global challenges—declared it a sacred sanctuary, a place where individuals could reconnect with their inner selves and rediscover their connection to the planet.

People from all corners of the Earth journeyed to the island, seeking solace, guidance, and inspiration. They immersed themselves in its lush forests, swam in its crystal-clear waters, and marveled at the vibrant tapestry of life that thrived within its boundaries. The island became a place of transformation, where individuals could heal their spirits and reignite their passion for protecting the Earth.

Amelia and Gabriel's descendants became the stewards of the island, forming a council dedicated to its preservation and fostering a deep understanding of its spiritual significance. They facilitated workshops, retreats, and gatherings that brought together diverse cultures, promoting peace, cooperation, and a shared commitment to environmental sustainability.

The island's unique energy also attracted researchers and scientists from various disciplines. They studied its extraordinary properties, unlocking new insights into the interconnectedness of all living beings and pioneering revolutionary advancements in fields like renewable energy, medicine, and consciousness exploration.

As the island's influence spread, its teachings and practices were integrated into global societies. Governments implemented policies rooted in sustainability and nature conservation, working hand in hand with local communities to protect and restore ecosystems worldwide. Renewable energy became the primary source of power, and innovative solutions for waste management and resource utilization became commonplace.

The world, now united in its dedication to the planet's well-being, witnessed a remarkable transformation. The detrimental impacts of past centuries were gradually reversed, and the Earth flourished with renewed vitality. Biodiversity thrived, oceans teemed with life, and the atmosphere cleansed itself of pollutants.

The island remained a beacon of hope, a sanctuary that reminded humanity of its interconnectedness and responsibility towards the Earth. It continued to attract people seeking enlightenment, solace, and guidance, as well as those on scientific quests to unravel its remaining mysteries.

And so, as time continued its eternal march, the island that once sheltered Amelia and Gabriel became a symbol of unity, resilience, and the indomitable human spirit. Their story, intertwined with the island's ancient energy, guided humanity towards a future where love, harmony, and sustainable coexistence with the Earth prevailed.

As generations carried their legacy forward, their names became immortalized in the annals of history, forever associated with the island's transformative power. The island, a testament to their incredible journey, stood as a testament to the limitless possibilities of the human spirit and the enduring impact of love, reminding humanity of its inherent connection to the natural world for ages to come.

In the distant future, a team of intrepid explorers embarked on a mission to search for new frontiers beyond the Earth. Equipped with advanced spacecraft and technology, they set their sights on distant galaxies, driven by an insatiable curiosity and a desire to push the boundaries of human knowledge.

During their interstellar voyage, the explorers stumbled upon a celestial anomaly—an interdimensional portal that transported them to a realm unlike anything they had ever encountered. As they emerged from the portal, they found themselves standing on an unfamiliar, lush and vibrant island, resonating with a powerful energy.

To their astonishment, they discovered that this was the same island where Amelia and Gabriel had spent 23 years stranded all those centuries ago. The island had been transformed, infused with mystical energies that transcended the boundaries of time and space.

The explorers, guided by their sense of adventure, curiosity, and a deep reverence for history, decided to explore the island further. As they ventured deeper into its verdant jungles and crystal-clear waters, they realized that the island possessed extraordinary abilities.

The island's energy could manipulate and shape reality, granting its inhabitants the power to manifest their intentions and desires. It was a place where dreams and imagination became tangible, where the laws of physics were fluid and malleable.

Realizing the potential of this newfound power, the explorers made a bold decision. They contacted Earth and informed humanity of their discovery, sharing the existence of the island and its transformative capabilities.

The news caused a global sensation. Governments, scientists, and individuals from all walks of life were captivated by the possibilities that the island held. Plans were set in motion to establish a permanent settlement, with the goal of harnessing the island's energies for the betterment of humanity.

cientists and engineers collaborated to develop technologies that could harness and responsibly utilize
ie island's power. The island became a hub of innovation, where groundbreaking advancements in
iergy, medicine, and consciousness exploration were pioneered.

eople from around the world flocked to the island, seeking to unlock their hidden potentials and tap
ito the limitless energy that surrounded them. The island became a melting pot of cultures, ideas, and
erspectives, fostering a global community united in their quest for knowledge and self-discovery.

s the island's influence spread, humanity experienced a profound transformation. The limitations of
ie past dissolved, and a new era of human potential began. Diseases that had plagued mankind for
enturies were cured, poverty and inequality were eradicated, and humanity reached unprecedented
evels of harmony and understanding.

melia and Gabriel, their story woven into the very fabric of the island, were revered as legendary
gures. Monuments and statues were erected in their honor, and their names became synonymous with
ourage, resilience, and the boundless possibilities of the human spirit.

he island, now a beacon of enlightenment and limitless potential, continued to be a source of
ispiration for generations to come. Its energy radiated throughout the cosmos, drawing curious souls
om distant star systems who sought to learn from its profound wisdom.

nd so, the island that once served as the backdrop to a tale of survival and longing became the
ateway to a new chapter in human history. Amelia and Gabriel's legacy, intertwined with the island's

thereal energies, guided humanity towards a future where the boundaries of reality were continuously
ushed, where dreams could be realized, and where the interconnectedness of all things was embraced.

s time unfolded, the island's story and the remarkable individuals who had graced its shores became a
egend that transcended the confines of the universe, etching their names among the stars and ensuring
iat their tale would be forever whispered in the annals of cosmic history.

s the explorers ventured deeper into the cosmos, their spacecraft traversed vast distances, carrying
iem to the far reaches of the universe. Their eyes were filled with wonder as they witnessed the
reathtaking beauty of distant galaxies, nebulae, and celestial phenomena.

)uring their journey, they turned their gaze back towards the pale blue dot they once called home—the
'arth. From the vastness of space, they marveled at its fragile beauty, suspended like a jewel in the vast
xpanse. They observed the swirling clouds, the intricate patterns of land and water, and the
himmering auroras that danced across its atmosphere.

rom their unique vantage point, the explorers could see the impact humanity had on their home planet.
'hey witnessed the lights of bustling cities, the interconnected networks of communication, and the
igns of technological advancements. Yet, they also witnessed the scars of environmental degradation
nd the consequences of unsustainable practices.

Motivated by their deep love for Earth and their newfound understanding of its interconnectedness with the cosmos, the explorers made a commitment. They vowed to bring back the knowledge they gained from their interstellar journey and use it to benefit their home planet.

Returning to Earth as ambassadors of the universe, the explorers shared their experiences, insights, and discoveries with scientists, leaders, and the global community. They inspired a new era of cosmic awareness and galvanized humanity to address the pressing challenges facing the planet.

Harnessing the knowledge gained from their interstellar voyage, humanity embarked on a collective mission to create a sustainable and harmonious future. Governments, organizations, and individuals around the world worked together to develop innovative solutions to tackle climate change, protect biodiversity, and promote social and economic equity.

Technological advancements soared to new heights. Clean and renewable energy sources became the norm, transforming the way societies powered their homes, transportation, and industries. Environmental restoration efforts flourished, reclaiming damaged ecosystems and revitalizing biodiversity.

Education and awareness initiatives spread across the globe, fostering a deep sense of responsibility and stewardship for the Earth. People from all walks of life engaged in sustainable practices, embracing a lifestyle that honored the delicate balance between humanity and the natural world.

The explorers themselves became influential figures, advocating for the protection of Earth's ecosystems and sharing the transformative power of space exploration. They collaborated with scientists, artists, and thought leaders to convey the profound interconnections that exist between the cosmos and life on Earth.

Through their efforts, a new era of environmental consciousness and cosmic perspective dawned. Humanity became custodians of the Earth, recognizing that its fate was intricately linked to the greater cosmic tapestry. As they looked back at the Earth from their space-faring vessels, they saw a planet healing, a world united, and a future brimming with hope.

And so, as time unfolded, the explorers' legacy remained etched in the stars, their journey a testament to the transformative power of space exploration. The collective efforts of humanity, inspired by their cosmic perspective, ensured that Earth thrived, not only as a home for humanity but as a precious jewel in the cosmos—a symbol of resilience, unity, and the enduring quest to understand and protect the wonders of the universe.

The spacecraft that carried the explorers on their interstellar voyage was a marvel of advanced technology and engineering. Designed for long-duration space travel, it possessed a sleek and aerodynamic exterior, allowing it to efficiently navigate through the vastness of the cosmos.

The ship's outer hull was made of a lightweight yet durable material that provided protection against micrometeoroids and cosmic radiation. Its surface shimmered with a metallic sheen, reflecting the brilliance of distant stars as it sailed through the celestial expanse.

The spacecraft featured large panoramic windows, allowing the explorers to gaze out into the depths of space, immersing themselves in the awe-inspiring views of galaxies, nebulas, and the vast cosmic tapestry. The glass was specially designed to withstand the extreme conditions of space, offering a clear and unobstructed view of the universe beyond.

Inside, the ship was a testament to both functionality and comfort. The central command center, located at the heart of the spacecraft, housed a wide array of advanced instruments and navigational systems. These cutting-edge technologies enabled precise course corrections, ensuring the explorers could navigate through the cosmic currents with accuracy.

Living quarters were designed with both practicality and coziness in mind. Sleeping compartments provided comfortable berths, equipped with adjustable harnesses to keep the explorers secure during periods of microgravity. Personal spaces were adorned with photographs, mementos, and reminders of home, fostering a sense of familiarity and connection amidst the vastness of space.

The ship's interior featured communal areas where the explorers could gather to share meals, engage in discussions, or simply enjoy moments of relaxation and camaraderie. These spaces were designed to foster a sense of community, allowing the explorers to bond and support each other throughout their journey.

The spacecraft was equipped with advanced life support systems that ensured the explorers had a constant supply of breathable air, purified water, and nutrient-rich food. Recycling technologies minimized waste and maximized resource efficiency, allowing the explorers to sustain themselves for extended periods without relying on resupply missions.

The ship's propulsion system employed advanced technologies, enabling it to achieve incredible speeds and traverse vast cosmic distances. Whether through the manipulation of exotic energy sources or the

harnessing of gravitational forces, the spacecraft propelled itself through space with grace and efficiency.

To maintain contact with Earth and other distant outposts, the ship was equipped with powerful communication arrays and relay systems. These technologies allowed the explorers to stay connected to their home planet, transmitting data, messages, and scientific discoveries back to humanity.

Overall, the spacecraft was a testament to human ingenuity, capable of withstanding the rigors of interstellar travel while providing a safe, comfortable, and awe-inspiring environment for the explorers. It represented the culmination of years of scientific advancement and technological breakthroughs, carrying humanity's hopes and dreams as it ventured into the uncharted realms of the cosmos.

On board the spacecraft, there were a total of six explorers, each with unique names and duties. Here are the names and roles of the crew members:

Captain Ava Rodriguez: Captain Rodriguez was a seasoned astronaut and skilled leader. She oversaw the entire mission, ensuring the safety and well-being of the crew, making critical decisions, and coordinating all operations aboard the spacecraft.

Dr. Ethan Park: Dr. Park was a brilliant astrophysicist and the chief science officer of the mission. His expertise in celestial mechanics and cosmology allowed him to navigate the complexities of interstellar travel and analyze the cosmic phenomena encountered during the journey.

Commander Maya Patel: Commander Patel was a skilled pilot and the spacecraft's primary navigator. With her exceptional piloting skills and extensive knowledge of spacecraft systems, she ensured precise maneuvering and calculated trajectories, guiding the ship through the vastness of space.

Dr. Amelia Collins: Dr. Collins was a renowned biologist and the ship's chief researcher. Her expertise in exobiology and astrobiology allowed her to study any extraterrestrial life forms or signs of habitable environments encountered during the voyage, unraveling the mysteries of life in the cosmos.

Engineer Marcus Chen: Engineer Chen was a master of spacecraft systems and maintenance. He was responsible for ensuring the smooth operation of all onboard systems, troubleshooting any technical issues, and overseeing repairs and upgrades to keep the spacecraft in optimal condition.

Communications Specialist Isabella Ramirez: Isabella Ramirez was a skilled communicator and linguist. Her role involved maintaining contact with Earth and other civilizations, deciphering and translating alien languages, and facilitating effective communication between the crew and any encountered sentient beings.

Together, this diverse team of explorers combined their knowledge, skills, and passion for discovery to navigate the cosmos, conduct scientific research, and represent the collective aspirations of humanity as they embarked on their interstellar journey.

The interstellar journey undertaken by the explorers was an epic undertaking, spanning a significant duration of time. It lasted for a total of 10 Earth years, accounting for the vast distances they had to cover and the complexities of interstellar travel.

To ensure the success of the mission, meticulous planning and preparation took place prior to the launch. The spacecraft was stocked with ample supplies, carefully calculated to sustain the crew throughout the entire duration of the journey. This included provisions such as food, water, and essential resources necessary for their survival and well-being.

Advanced technologies were employed to maximize resource efficiency and recycling onboard the spacecraft. Life support systems were designed to continuously provide breathable air, purify water, and recycle waste, minimizing the need for resupply missions and reducing their reliance on external resources.

The crew also carried out regular maintenance and repairs to ensure the spacecraft's systems remained functional and efficient throughout the voyage. Their expertise in various fields, including engineering and life sciences, allowed them to address any technical issues that arose during the mission.

Additionally, the explorers had access to state-of-the-art laboratories and research facilities within the spacecraft. These facilities allowed them to conduct scientific experiments, analyze data, and make significant discoveries during their journey.

While the voyage was undoubtedly challenging and required careful resource management, the explorers had taken every precaution to ensure they had enough supplies and equipment to sustain them throughout the entirety of the ten-year interstellar trip

During their ten-year interstellar journey, the explorers encountered several challenges and obstacles that required them to solve a number of errors and issues. These errors varied in nature and complexity, requiring the crew to draw upon their expertise and problem-solving skills to overcome them. Here are a few examples:

1. Navigation Errors: Navigating through the vastness of space presented numerous challenges, including gravitational anomalies, celestial bodies, and unknown phenomena. The crew had to continually adjust their course and make precise calculations to ensure they stayed on track and avoided collisions or gravitational disruptions.

2. Technical Malfunctions: Despite meticulous planning and preparation, technical malfunctions could still occur during the long journey. These could include failures in critical systems, such as life support, communication, or propulsion. The crew had to troubleshoot and repair these malfunctions to ensure the spacecraft's continued operation and the safety of the crew.

3. Resource Management: The limited resources onboard the spacecraft required careful management and conservation. The crew had to monitor supplies such as food, water, and fuel, calculating consumption rates and implementing strategies to maximize resource efficiency and minimize waste.

4. Psychological Challenges: Extended isolation and confinement in space could pose psychological challenges for the crew. They had to maintain their mental well-being, manage stress, and ensure effective teamwork and communication throughout the journey. Strategies such as regular communication with mission control on Earth, recreational activities, and psychological support systems were implemented to address these challenges.

5. Data Analysis and Interpretation: The explorers encountered various cosmic phenomena and collected vast amounts of data during their journey. Analyzing and interpreting this data accurately was crucial for their scientific research and understanding of the universe. They had to develop algorithms, models, and analytical techniques to extract meaningful insights from the data they collected.

6. Unknown Encounters: As they ventured into uncharted territories, the crew encountered unknown phenomena, alien species, or potentially hazardous situations. They had to employ their scientific expertise and diplomatic skills to navigate these encounters safely and learn from them.

While these errors and challenges posed difficulties, the crew's expertise, collaboration, and determination allowed them to solve these problems, learn from them, and adapt to the demands of the interstellar journey. Each obstacle they faced provided an opportunity for growth, resilience, and further exploration of the mysteries of the cosmos.

During their interstellar journey, the explorers encountered several alien spacecraft, each belonging to different extraterrestrial civilizations. Here are the names of the alien ships they observed:

1. Celestial Dawn: The explorers came across a sleek, silver vessel with a smooth, aerodynamic design. This ship, known as the Celestial Dawn, was operated by a highly advanced and peaceful civilization that had achieved remarkable technological advancements.

2. Nebula Wanderer: Another encounter led the explorers to witness a massive spacecraft, resembling a floating celestial body. This ship, called the Nebula Wanderer, belonged to a nomadic species that roamed the cosmos, exploring different galaxies and star systems.

3. Harmonic Radiance: In a distant star system, the explorers observed a strikingly beautiful spacecraft named the Harmonic Radiance. It emanated soft, multicolored lights, accompanied by harmonic frequencies that reverberated through space. The ship was piloted by a species with a deep connection to music and sound.

4. Luminescent Starfire: A brief encounter with a swift and agile ship named the Luminescent Starfire left the explorers in awe. This vessel belonged to a highly advanced race that harnessed energy from stars to power their spacecraft, giving it a radiant glow as it soared through space.

5. Enigma Seraph: The explorers came across a mysterious ship known as the Enigma Seraph, which defied conventional design. Its shape constantly shifted and morphed, adapting to its surroundings. The beings piloting this vessel were enigmatic and possessed advanced knowledge of cosmic phenomena.

It is important to note that the encounters and names provided are purely fictional, as our current knowledge and understanding of extraterrestrial life and their spacecraft are limited. However, in the realm of imagination and science fiction, these names represent the sense of wonder and diversity that could exist in a universe teeming with life.

During their interstellar journey, the explorers made attempts to establish communication with the alien civilizations they encountered. While the specifics of the communications and the information exchanged would depend on the nature of each encounter, here are some possibilities of what they might have learned through these communications:

1. Introductions and Greetings: The explorers and the alien beings would have exchanged basic greetings and introductions, attempting to establish a common ground for communication.

2. Cultural Exchange: The explorers and the aliens may have shared information about their respective cultures, customs, and histories, allowing for a mutual understanding and appreciation of each other's backgrounds.

3. Technological Insights: The explorers might have gained valuable insights into the advanced technologies employed by the alien civilizations, potentially leading to new scientific discoveries and advancements for humanity.

4. Scientific Knowledge: Through communication, the explorers and the alien beings could have shared scientific knowledge and discoveries, deepening the understanding of the universe and potentially unveiling new cosmic phenomena or principles.

5. Cosmic Wisdom: The alien civilizations might have imparted profound insights and wisdom about the nature of the cosmos, its interconnectedness, and the existence of other intelligent life forms, expanding the explorers' perspective and challenging their preconceived notions.

6. Environmental and Ecological Perspectives: The explorers and the aliens might have exchanged information about their respective planets' environments, ecosystems, and the ways in which they sustain life. This knowledge could have profound implications for Earth's own environmental challenges and conservation efforts.

. Philosophical and Existential Discussions: Communication with advanced civilizations could have ed to deep philosophical and existential discussions about the nature of existence, consciousness, and he purpose of life. These exchanges might have offered the explorers new perspectives and prompted rofound introspection.

 is important to note that these potential outcomes are speculative and based on the imagination and he realm of science fiction. The nature of interstellar communication and the actual content of these xchanges, if they were to occur, remain uncertain until we have concrete evidence of extraterrestrial fe and the ability to establish direct contact.

fter the explorers came aboard the alien ship, they found themselves in a truly extraordinary nvironment. The interior of the alien vessel was a fascinating blend of advanced technology, nfamiliar aesthetics, and intriguing architectural designs.

1. Welcoming Committee: As the explorers stepped onto the alien ship, they were greeted by a delegation of alien beings. These beings, representing the crew or the leadership of the ship, extended a warm welcome and expressed their curiosity and interest in the human visitors.

2. Cultural Exchange: The explorers and the aliens engaged in a cultural exchange, sharing information about their respective societies, customs, and traditions. This exchange allowed for a deeper understanding and appreciation of each other's backgrounds and fostered a sense of connection and friendship.

3. Advanced Technology: The explorers were amazed by the advanced technology present on the alien ship. They had the opportunity to witness and learn about revolutionary scientific advancements, innovative propulsion systems, and sophisticated life support systems that surpassed anything humanity had achieved.

4. Cosmic Knowledge: The alien crew shared their profound knowledge about the universe, its mysteries, and their own experiences in the cosmos. The explorers were exposed to new scientific theories, cosmological insights, and perspectives that challenged their understanding of the universe.

5. Research Collaboration: The explorers and the alien crew had the chance to collaborate on scientific research projects. They shared data, analyzed cosmic phenomena together, and worked on unraveling the mysteries of the universe. This collaboration led to groundbreaking discoveries and expanded the frontiers of human knowledge.

6. Interpersonal Connections: Beyond the scientific and intellectual exchange, personal connections were formed between the explorers and the aliens. Friendships developed, cultural exchanges took place, and both parties gained a deeper appreciation for the shared experiences and commonalities that existed despite their differences.

7. Farewell and Continued Exploration: After a period of mutual learning and exploration, the time came for the explorers to bid farewell to their alien hosts. Both sides expressed gratitude for the enriching experience and exchanged promises to maintain contact and continue their exploration of the cosmos.

Upon leaving the alien ship, the explorers returned to their own spacecraft, carrying with them newfound knowledge, scientific breakthroughs, and cherished memories of the extraordinary encounter. Their interstellar journey continued, fueled by the inspiration and wonder that came from their brief but profound interaction with a civilization from another world, we met the alines.

1. Xal'thar: The leader of the alien crew, known for their wisdom and guidance.

2. Vyxara: A scientist from the alien species, renowned for their expertise in cosmic phenomena.

3. Zephyrion: A skilled engineer responsible for the advanced technology on the alien ship.

4. Lyra'thia: A diplomat and cultural liaison, facilitating communication and understanding between the human explorers and the alien crew.

5. Azurina: A botanist specializing in extraterrestrial flora and the study of alien ecosystems.

6. Nixtral: An astrophysicist with an in-depth understanding of the universe's mysteries and celestial mechanics.

Verdant Lumians: These aliens possess a vibrant green hue that covers their entire body. Their skin is smooth and iridescent, reflecting light in a captivating manner. They have slender, elongated bodies with a graceful physique. Lumians are known for their large, expressive eyes that shimmer with a radiant glow.

As the aliens embark on their journey toward Earth, their intentions can vary depending on what they want to explore. Here are a few possible motivations for their visit:

1. Azure Vortrans: In contrast to the Lumians, the Vortrans have a bluish-green skin tone that resemble the depths of a tranquil ocean. Their bodies are robust and muscular, adapted for physical endurance and agility. Vortrans possess bioluminescent patterns on their skin, which illuminate in intricate patterns during moments of excitement or communication.

1. Diplomatic Exchange: The aliens seek to establish diplomatic relations with Earth and foster interstellar cooperation. They aim to promote cultural exchange, scientific collaboration, and mutual understanding between their civilization and humanity.

2. Scientific Exploration: The aliens are driven by a thirst for knowledge and a desire to study Earth and its diverse ecosystems. They seek to learn about Earth's biodiversity, geology, and the complexities of human civilization. Their intention is purely scientific and driven by a curiosity to expand their understanding of the universe.

3. Resource Acquisition: The aliens have identified Earth as a potential source of valuable resources that are scarce or unavailable in their own solar system. Their intent is to engage in trade or resource extraction agreements, aiming to meet the needs of their civilization and maintain their technological advancement.

4. Humanitarian Assistance: The aliens have detected signals of distress or have been monitoring Earth's challenges, such as environmental crises or social conflicts. They arrive with the intention of providing assistance, sharing their advanced technologies, and helping humanity overcome these challenges.

5. First Contact and Observation: The aliens are on a mission of exploration and discovery. They want to make first contact with Earth to observe and study humanity, its behaviors, and its development as an intelligent species. Their intention is to learn about Earth's sociocultural dynamics and contribute to the galactic knowledge of intelligent life.

6. Warning or Intervention: The aliens have detected a looming threat or imminent danger that could impact Earth. They arrive with the intention of warning humanity or intervening to prevent a catastrophe, leveraging their advanced technology and knowledge to aid in averting potential disaster.

Emilia and Gabriel's children

As the years went by, Emilia and Gabriel's children grew into remarkable individuals, each forging their own path in the world of interstellar exploration and beyond. Their combined efforts and shared legacy continued to shape the future of humanity's relationship with the cosmos.

Sophia, with her deep curiosity and passion for astrophysics, became a renowned researcher, dedicated to unraveling the secrets of the universe. Through her groundbreaking discoveries, she expanded our understanding of cosmic phenomena, shedding light on the mysteries of black holes and the nature of dark matter.

Olivia, inspired by her parents' commitment to cultural integration, pursued a career as an intercultural ambassador. With her diplomatic skills and deep respect for diverse civilizations, she played a vital role in fostering interstellar cooperation and understanding, bringing Earth and alien civilizations closer together.

Ethan, driven by his love for space engineering, spearheaded groundbreaking projects in spacecraft design and propulsion systems. His innovative technologies revolutionized space travel, enabling humanity to reach farther into the cosmos and explore previously uncharted territories.

Isabella, with her passion for astrobiology, dedicated her life to the search for extraterrestrial life forms. Through her pioneering research, she discovered microbial organisms thriving in extreme environments on distant moons, providing crucial insights into the potential for life beyond Earth.

Alexander, guided by his parents' emphasis on ethical exploration, championed responsible space initiatives. As an advocate for sustainable practices, he worked tirelessly to ensure that humanity's interstellar endeavors prioritized the protection of alien ecosystems and the preservation of cosmic biodiversity.

Emily, drawn to the intersection of science and policy, became a leading voice in interstellar ethics and governance. Through her work in international organizations, she shaped policies and guidelines for

the ethical exploration and utilization of resources in space, ensuring a harmonious and sustainable future for all.

As the children pursued their respective paths, they often collaborated, combining their expertise to tackle complex challenges at the intersection of science, culture, and ethics. Together, they continued their parents' mission to expand human knowledge, deepen interstellar connections, and safeguard the integrity of the universe.

Their contributions propelled humanity to new heights, fostering a profound appreciation for the wonders of the cosmos and cultivating a sense of unity among diverse civilizations. Emilia and Gabriel's children, driven by their shared legacy and guided by their parents' wisdom, became beacons of hope, pushing the boundaries of what humanity could achieve in its quest to understand the universe and its place within it.

And so, as the story of Emilia and Gabriel's children unfolded, their collective efforts echoed through the cosmos, leaving an indelible mark on humanity's interstellar journey and inspiring generations to

come. The legacy they built would forever be remembered as a testament to the power of exploration, knowledge, and the enduring human spirit.

Emilia and Gabriel's children to have friends who share their interests and pursuits in the field of interstellar exploration. These friends could be individuals who have also been inspired by their parents' work or who have independently developed a passion for space exploration and scientific inquiry.

These like-minded friends might come from diverse backgrounds and cultures, representing a global community of young scientists, engineers, diplomats, and researchers who are dedicated to advancing our understanding of the universe and fostering interstellar connections. Together, they could form a supportive network, collaborating on projects, sharing knowledge and ideas, and pushing the boundaries of human exploration.

Through their shared experiences and friendships, Emilia and Gabriel's children would not only find companionship but also build a community of individuals who are collectively shaping the future of interstellar exploration and discovery. Their shared pursuits would foster collaboration, innovation, and the exchange of ideas, propelling humanity's journey into the cosmos forward

As time goes on, Emilia's children will continue to explore as their ancestors did.

Embarking on a journey to the center of the Earth is a monumental undertaking, and the activities that Emilia and Gabriel's children would engage in during this adventure would be filled with scientific exploration and discovery. Here are some possible activities they might undertake:

1. Geological Surveys: As they descend deeper into the Earth's layers, the children would conduct detailed geological surveys, studying the composition, structure, and seismic activity of the Earth's crust, mantle, and core. They would collect samples, analyze rock formations, and document their findings to deepen our understanding of the planet's internal dynamics.

2. Mapping and Cartography: The children would create detailed maps and three-dimensional models of the Earth's interior, charting the intricate network of underground tunnels, caverns, and geological features they encounter. This mapping effort would provide valuable insights into the planet's geology and aid in future scientific endeavors.

3. Environmental Monitoring: Along their journey, the children would monitor environmental conditions such as temperature, pressure, and chemical composition. By collecting data at various depths, they could observe how these parameters change and gain insights into the Earth's thermal and chemical processes.

4. Study of Subterranean Life: The children might encounter unique forms of subterranean life in the depths of the Earth. They would document and study these organisms, examining their adaptations to extreme conditions and their potential significance to the understanding of life's resilience and diversity.

5. Seismic Investigations: Equipped with specialized instruments, the children would measure and analyze seismic activity within the Earth. They would study earthquake patterns, analyze the

propagation of seismic waves, and gain insights into the tectonic forces that shape the planet's surface.

6. Exploration of Underground Caverns and Water Systems: As they navigate through underground caverns and water systems, the children would document the intricate beauty and complexity of these hidden landscapes. They would study the hydrological processes, examine underground rivers and lakes, and investigate the role of water in shaping the Earth's subsurface.

7. Uncovering Geological Mysteries: Throughout their journey, the children would encounter geological anomalies and phenomena that defy current understanding. They would investigate these mysteries, formulating hypotheses and conducting experiments to unravel the secrets hidden within the Earth's depths.

Their expedition to the center of the Earth would push the boundaries of human knowledge, shedding light on the planet's inner workings and revealing new insights into Earth's geological history and processes. The discoveries made by Emilia and Gabriel's children during this extraordinary journey would expand our understanding of our own planet and pave the way for future scientific advancements.

As their parents they were always on the go, next in Mars.

As Emilia and Gabriel's children embarked on their monumental journey to Mars, their efforts garnered global attention and inspired generations to dream of interplanetary exploration. Their mission to the red planet captivated the imaginations of people around the world, igniting a new era of scientific discovery and pushing the boundaries of human capabilities.

Throughout their expedition, the children encountered breathtaking landscapes, conducted groundbreaking research, and made significant strides in unraveling the mysteries of Mars. They

discovered evidence of ancient riverbeds, indicating the presence of water in Mars' distant past. They analyzed the Martian atmosphere, uncovering valuable insights into its composition and dynamics. And, to their astonishment, they even found microscopic signs of microbial life in the Martian soil, marking a historic milestone in the search for extraterrestrial life.

Their findings revolutionized our understanding of Mars and fueled a renewed determination to explore the cosmos. Scientists and engineers around the world built upon their research, developing technologies and strategies for sustainable colonization of the red planet. Collaborative efforts among international space agencies led to the establishment of permanent research bases, laying the groundwork for the eventual human settlement of Mars.

As the years passed, Emilia and Gabriel's children became revered figures in the scientific community, serving as ambassadors of interstellar exploration. Their knowledge and experiences were shared through books, documentaries, and educational programs, inspiring countless individuals to pursue careers in space science and engineering. They became advocates for responsible and ethical exploration, emphasizing the importance of preserving the integrity of celestial bodies and respecting the potential for extraterrestrial life.

The legacy of Emilia and Gabriel's children extended far beyond their groundbreaking discoveries on Mars. Their passion for exploration and their dedication to understanding the universe ignited a spark in humanity that continued to burn brightly. Their journey paved the way for future generations, who built upon their achievements, expanded humanity's reach in space, and forged connections with other intelligent civilizations in the cosmos.

As time went on, Emilia and Gabriel's children watched with pride as humanity ventured farther into the depths of space, driven by the insatiable curiosity that they had inherited from their parents. The boundless possibilities of interstellar exploration became a reality, forever transforming the destiny of our species.

And so, the story of Emilia and Gabriel's children came to a close, leaving a profound legacy that echoed through the annals of history. Their journey to Mars and their contributions to the realm of interstellar exploration ensured that humanity's thirst for knowledge, discovery, and connection with the cosmos would never be extinguished. They became true pioneers, leaving an indelible mark on the universe and inspiring generations to reach for the stars.

# Emily the Witch

Once upon a time, in the sleepy town of Hollowbrook, there lived a young girl named Emily. Emily possessed a unique and mysterious ability: she could see dead people. This extraordinary gift had haunted her since childhood, presenting her with a constant connection to the spirit realm. However, there was one peculiar condition tied to her power; she could only see these apparitions in complete darkness.

Emily was a brave and curious soul, undeterred by the chilling encounters she faced each day. While most people would dread the idea of walking in the dark, she sought solace in the eerie glow of moonl. nights and the profound silence that accompanied them.

One fateful evening, a solar eclipse descended upon Hollowbrook, casting an eerie shadow over the town. The entire place was cloaked in darkness as the moon blocked the sun's radiant light. Emily knew that this was her chance to venture into a realm that existed between the living and the dead, where secrets lay shrouded and spirits roamed freely.

As the sun's last ray succumbed to darkness, Emily stepped out onto the deserted streets, feeling the presence of souls lingering around her. Wisps of ethereal figures emerged, whispering in voices only she could hear. They sought her assistance, longing for a connection to the world they had left behind.

Guided by an otherworldly force, Emily embarked on a quest to fulfill the desires of these restless spirits. With each encounter, she learned more about their unfinished business and the unresolved mysteries that kept them tethered to the earthly plane.

Amidst her spectral encounters, Emily stumbled upon a particularly tormented spirit named Samuel. Samuel, a lost soul trapped between worlds, had been searching for his missing daughter for decades. Determined to bring peace to both the living and the dead, Emily vowed to help Samuel unravel the truth behind his daughter's disappearance.

Together, Emily and Samuel embarked on a treacherous journey through Hollowbrook's forgotten history. As they delved deeper into the town's secrets, they uncovered a hidden underworld of corruption, deceit, and unspeakable crimes. Emily's ability to communicate with the dead became invaluable, as the spirits provided her with clues and insights that no living being could ever possess.

With the darkness as their ally, Emily and Samuel unveiled a web of treachery that reached high into the town's ranks, implicating influential individuals who had long evaded justice. In their pursuit of truth, they risked their own safety, navigating through a dangerous labyrinth of darkness and deception

As the solar eclipse slowly waned, revealing the return of light, Emily and Samuel finally uncovered the shocking truth behind Samuel's daughter's disappearance. The revelation not only freed Samuel's spirit, but it also brought justice to the living and the dead.

Emily's extraordinary gift, once viewed as a curse, had become a powerful tool to bring closure to those who had lost their way. Hollowbrook, forever changed by the events that unfolded during that eclipsed night, found solace in the knowledge that no secret could remain hidden in the dark forever.

And so, Emily continued her journey, walking alongside spirits in the moonlit nights, aiding those in need and shedding light on the darkest corners of existence, knowing that her ability to see dead people would forever be her guiding light

In the aftermath of the eclipse, the tale of Emily's extraordinary abilities spread throughout Hollowbrook and beyond. People were fascinated and intrigued by her unique connection to the spirit world. Some admired her bravery, while others feared the unknown and the power she held.

Emily's newfound fame attracted the attention of a renowned paranormal researcher named Dr. Benjamin Hartley. Driven by a desire to understand the mysteries of the afterlife, he sought out Emily, eager to study her abilities and unravel the secrets of her gift.

Initially hesitant, Emily eventually agreed to collaborate with Dr. Hartley, recognizing the potential to learn more about her powers and perhaps discover a way to control or enhance them. Together, they embarked on a series of experiments and investigations into the supernatural.

Their partnership led them to various haunted locations, where Emily's ability to see and communicate with spirits proved invaluable. They ventured into abandoned asylums, haunted mansions, and ancient burial grounds, documenting their encounters and collecting evidence of the spirit realm.

As their research progressed, Emily and Dr. Hartley encountered both benevolent and malevolent spirits, delving into the depths of the paranormal world. They encountered vengeful ghosts seeking retribution, lost souls longing for closure, and even benevolent spirits guiding them towards forgotten truths.

Their collaborative efforts not only expanded humanity's understanding of the afterlife but also provided comfort and closure to countless spirits and their loved ones. Emily's unique perspective and compassion allowed her to bridge the gap between the living and the dead, offering solace and resolution to those who had long been forgotten.

Throughout their endeavors, Emily and Dr. Hartley formed a deep bond, blending their knowledge and skills to create a profound partnership. They became pioneers in the field of paranormal research, authoring numerous books and presenting their findings at conferences worldwide.

Emily's journey not only brought her personal growth but also ignited a global fascination with the supernatural. She became a symbol of hope for those seeking answers about life after death and a source of inspiration for others who felt different or misunderstood.

As time went on, Emily's abilities continued to evolve. She discovered new facets of her gift, including the ability to sense emotions and energies in her surroundings. With each passing day, she honed her skills, determined to push the boundaries of what was known about the spirit world.

Emily's story served as a reminder that sometimes the darkest parts of our existence hold the greatest mysteries and the most profound connections. She became a beacon of light for those who found themselves lost in the shadows, reminding them that even in the darkest of nights, there is always a glimmer of hope and a chance for understanding.

And so, Emily's journey continued, with each step revealing new revelations, unraveling enigmatic secrets, and shining a light on the invisible threads that connect the realms of the living and the dead.

As Emily's journey unfolded, her reputation as a renowned paranormal investigator grew, and she attracted the attention of a secret society known as The Seekers. The Seekers were a clandestine organization dedicated to understanding and harnessing supernatural abilities for the betterment of humankind.

Intrigued by Emily's unique connection to the spirit world, The Seekers approached her with an offer to join their ranks. Recognizing the potential to further explore and refine her powers, Emily agreed, eager to delve deeper into the mysteries that had defined her life.

Within The Seekers, Emily found a community of individuals with extraordinary gifts, each bringing their own expertise to the table. They shared knowledge, trained together, and undertook missions that involved investigating paranormal phenomena around the world.

Emily's enhanced abilities allowed her to penetrate the depths of the supernatural like never before. She became adept at not only communicating with spirits but also manipulating and channeling spiritual energy. With guidance from her newfound allies, she learned to protect herself from malevolent entities and use her powers for the greater good.

As part of The Seekers, Emily and her team were called upon to investigate cases of spiritual unrest, hauntings, and mysterious occurrences that baffled both the scientific and spiritual communities. They traveled to ancient ruins, cursed locations, and even explored the depths of the spirit realm itself, seeking answers to age-old questions about the nature of life, death, and the afterlife.

Through their missions, Emily and The Seekers unearthed ancient artifacts, deciphered cryptic symbols, and pieced together fragments of forgotten lore. Their discoveries expanded humanity's understanding of the supernatural, rewriting the boundaries of what was deemed possible.

However, not all was as it seemed within The Seekers. Emily began to uncover a darker side to the organization, as certain members sought to exploit their powers for personal gain. Betrayal and intrigue clouded their once unified cause, threatening to tear the group apart.

Determined to protect the sanctity of their mission, Emily led a group of loyal Seekers in a rebellion against those who had strayed from the path of integrity. The ensuing conflict tested their abilities, alliances, and moral compasses.

In the midst of the internal strife, an ancient prophecy came to light, foretelling a cataclysmic event that could tip the balance between the realms of the living and the dead. The fate of both worlds hung in the balance, and Emily realized that she held the key to averting the impending disaster.

With the trust of her loyal allies and her unwavering determination, Emily embarked on a perilous quest to uncover the truth behind the prophecy and find a way to prevent the catastrophic event from occurring. The journey took her to the far corners of the globe and deep into the heart of the spirit realm, where she confronted powerful entities and faced her own deepest fears.

In a climactic battle, Emily embraced her true potential, harnessing her abilities to bridge the gap between the living and the dead. With the support of her allies, she successfully thwarted the prophecy, restoring balance to both worlds.

Having fulfilled her destiny, Emily chose to retire from active duty, opting for a quieter life. She settled in a secluded corner of the world, offering guidance to those who sought her help and sharing her vast knowledge with a select few. Her legacy lived on, inspiring a new generation of seekers and igniting a greater understanding and acceptance of the supernatural.

And so, Emily's extraordinary journey came to a close, leaving a lasting impact on the realms of the living and the dead. Her story became a legend, whispered in hushed tones by those who dared to believe in the extraordinary. And while the darkness continued to hold its secrets, Emily's indomitable spirit reminded the world that there was always light to be found, even in the most obscure corners of existence.

One personal aspect of Emily's life was her deep love for music. From a young age, she found solace and inspiration in the melodies and lyrics that resonated with her soul. Music became a powerful outlet for her emotions, a means of expression that went beyond words.

Emily possessed a beautiful singing voice and often retreated to her room, where she would lose herself in the melodies that flowed from her lips. Whether it was classical compositions, soulful ballads, or hauntingly ethereal tunes, she poured her heart into every note.

In times of uncertainty or distress, Emily would seek comfort in the embrace of her music. She found that singing allowed her to connect with her own emotions and offered a cathartic release from the

weight of her extraordinary abilities. It was a personal sanctuary where she could be vulnerable and let her spirit soar.

Emily's love for music extended beyond her private moments. She occasionally performed at local coffee shops and small venues, captivating audiences with her enchanting voice. Her performances became a window into her soul, as her haunting melodies and heartfelt lyrics resonated deeply with those who listened.

Despite her gift to see the dead and the darkness that often accompanied it, Emily found solace and healing through the power of music. It served as a reminder of the beauty that could be found even in the darkest corners of existence, and it connected her to the raw emotions that made her feel truly alive.

Despite her gift to see the dead and the darkness that often accompanied her, Emily possessed an unwavering sense of empathy and compassion. She recognized that the spirits she encountered were not mere specters, but remnants of once vibrant lives. Emily made it her personal mission to bring solace and closure to these lost souls.

With each encounter, Emily took the time to listen to the stories of the departed, offering them a sympathetic ear and a comforting presence. She understood that they were trapped in a liminal space, yearning for resolution or a connection to the world they had left behind.

Emily dedicated countless hours to helping these spirits find peace, using her unique ability to communicate with them to guide them towards the light. She believed that no soul deserved to linger in a state of unrest, and she tirelessly worked to reconcile the unfinished business that held them back.

Beyond her interactions with the supernatural, Emily's empathy extended to the living as well. She had a profound understanding of the pain and struggles that people faced, and she became a pillar of support for those who sought her guidance. Her ability to see beyond the surface and truly connect with others allowed her to offer profound insights and comfort in their times of need.

Even in her own moments of darkness and personal challenges, Emily remained a beacon of compassion. She never allowed the weight of her gift to overshadow her innate kindness and understanding. Instead, she channeled her experiences into fuel for her determination to make a difference in the lives of both the living and the dead.

Emily's unwavering empathy became a defining aspect of her character. It was her ability to see the pain in others and offer a compassionate hand that touched the lives of many, leaving a lasting impact on all who had the privilege of crossing paths with her

Beyond her interactions with the supernatural and her ability to see the dead, Emily had another secret: she was a witch. Deep within her lineage, she carried the blood of powerful witches who had come before her, and she embraced her magical heritage with reverence and awe.

From a young age, Emily displayed a natural affinity for the mystical arts. She possessed an inherent connection to the elements and an intuitive understanding of the unseen forces that shaped the world around her. Her gift for witchcraft complemented her ability to see and communicate with spirits, allowing her to navigate both the physical and spiritual realms with ease.

In the seclusion of her home, Emily immersed herself in the study of ancient grimoires, potions, and incantations. She practiced the craft diligently, honing her skills in spellcasting, divination, and the manipulation of energy. Her rituals were a blend of tradition and personal intuition, guided by a deep respect for the natural balance of the universe.

Emily's witchcraft became an integral part of her mission to help spirits find peace. She utilized her magical abilities to create protective wards, banish malevolent entities, and create sacred spaces where lost souls could find solace. Her spells and rituals were tools of healing and restoration, bridging the gap between the living and the dead.

In addition to her work with spirits, Emily embraced her role as a healer and advisor to her community. People sought her out for remedies, spiritual guidance, and even the occasional love potion. She used

er magical knowledge to bring harmony and transformation into the lives of those who crossed her
ath.

Iowever, Emily also understood the responsibility and potential dangers that came with her powers.
he adhered to a strict code of ethics, using her magic for the greater good and always mindful of the
onsequences of her actions. She believed in maintaining the delicate balance between the natural and
upernatural realms, never overstepping the boundaries of free will or disrupting the cosmic order.

)espite the secrecy surrounding her witchcraft, Emily's magical abilities and her connection to the
upernatural fueled her journey. They provided her with the tools to navigate the darkest corners of
xistence and to offer a glimmer of hope and healing to both the living and the dead.

:mily's duality as a witch who could see dead people in the dark made her an even more enigmatic
igure, adding layers of mystery and power to her already extraordinary story. She became a beacon of
1agic, reminding the world of the ancient wisdom that flowed through her veins and the transformative
otential that resided within each individual who dared to embrace their true nature.

:mily's path as a witch was guided by a strong moral compass and a genuine desire to help others. She
arnessed her magical abilities for the betterment of humanity and the spiritual realm.

\s a good witch, Emily used her powers to heal the wounded, bring comfort to the afflicted, and offer
uidance to those in need. Her spells and rituals were crafted with positive intentions, focusing on love,
ght, and restoration. She believed in the power of magic to bring about positive change and worked
iligently to make a difference in the lives of those she encountered.

:mily's reputation as a kind and benevolent witch spread throughout her community. People sought her
ut not only for her ability to communicate with spirits but also for her magical expertise. She became
nown as a trusted advisor, offering practical solutions and enchanted remedies to those who sought her
ssistance.

Ier magical prowess extended beyond the realms of healing. Emily used her witchcraft to protect the
ulnerable, ward off negative energies, and promote harmony in her community. Whether it was
hrough protective spells for homes or empowering charms for individuals, she employed her magical
alents to create a safer and more balanced environment for those around her.

'urthermore, Emily embraced her role as a teacher and mentor to aspiring witches. She recognized the
mportance of passing on her knowledge and ensuring that the practice of magic remained in capable
nd responsible hands. She guided and nurtured the talents of young witches, emphasizing the
mportance of ethics, respect, and the responsible use of magic.

'hroughout her journey, Emily remained true to her principles and used her magical abilities as a force
or good. Her actions touched the lives of many, leaving behind a legacy of compassion, healing, and
ositive change. She exemplified the true essence of a good witch, standing as a testament to the
ransformative power of magic when wielded with wisdom and integrity.

Emily's path as a witch was guided by a strong moral compass and a genuine desire to help others. She harnessed her magical abilities for the betterment of humanity and the spiritual realm.

As a good witch, Emily used her powers to heal the wounded, bring comfort to the afflicted, and offer guidance to those in need. Her spells and rituals were crafted with positive intentions, focusing on

love, light, and restoration. She believed in the power of magic to bring about positive change and worked diligently to make a difference in the lives of those she encountered.

Emily's reputation as a kind and benevolent witch spread throughout her community. People sought her out not only for her ability to communicate with spirits but also for her magical expertise. She became known as a trusted advisor, offering practical solutions and enchanted remedies to those who sought her assistance.

Her magical prowess extended beyond the realms of healing. Emily used her witchcraft to protect the vulnerable, ward off negative energies, and promote harmony in her community. Whether it was through protective spells for homes or empowering charms for individuals, she employed her magical talents to create a safer and more balanced environment for those around her.

Furthermore, Emily embraced her role as a teacher and mentor to aspiring witches. She recognized the importance of passing on her knowledge and ensuring that the practice of magic remained in capable and responsible hands. She guided and nurtured the talents of young witches, emphasizing the importance of ethics, respect, and the responsible use of magic.

Throughout her journey, Emily remained true to her principles and used her magical abilities as a force for good. Her actions touched the lives of many, leaving behind a legacy of compassion, healing, and positive change. She exemplified the true essence of a good witch, standing as a testament to the transformative power of magic when wielded with wisdom and integrity.

Indeed, as a witch with extraordinary powers, Emily possessed the ability to manipulate objects with her mind. Known as telekinesis, this gift allowed her to move and control physical objects without any physical contact. Whether it was levitating small items or rearranging furniture, Emily's telekinetic abilities added another layer of intrigue to her magical repertoire.

When it came to her personal preferences, Emily had a fondness for enjoying a glass of wine. In moments of relaxation or celebration, she would savor the flavors and aromas of the fermented grape

beverage. Wine became a symbolic indulgence for her, representing the appreciation of life's pleasures and the interconnectedness of the physical and spiritual realms.

In her quiet moments, Emily would sometimes combine her love for music, magic, and wine, creating enchanting rituals that celebrated the harmony between these elements. She would light candles, pour a glass of her favorite vintage, and allow the melodies she sang or played on her instruments to weave a spell of ambiance and serenity.

The act of enjoying wine held a deeper significance for Emily. It symbolized the balance between the mundane and the magical, reminding her to find joy and inspiration in the simple pleasures of everyday life. It was a reminder that while she possessed extraordinary gifts, she was also human, capable of experiencing the richness of the world in all its sensory delights.

So, in the midst of her journey as a witch, Emily found moments to savor a glass of wine, allowing it to be a source of relaxation, inspiration, and a connection to her own humanity. It served as a reminder

that even amidst the extraordinary, the simple pleasures of life remained an essential part of her existence.

During her trance states, Emily's connection to the spiritual realm deepened, allowing her to perceive mystical creatures that existed beyond the realm of ordinary human perception. Among these extraordinary beings, dragons held a prominent place in her visionary experiences.

As her consciousness transcended the physical plane, Emily would encounter majestic dragons in their ethereal form. These powerful creatures, with their scales gleaming like precious gems and wings spanning vast distances, captivated her with their grace and ancient wisdom. Dragons represented a symbol of strength, knowledge, and elemental forces, serving as guardians of hidden realms and keepers of ancient secrets.

Beyond dragons, Emily's trance states also unveiled a rich tapestry of other mystical creatures. She would encounter magnificent unicorns, with their pure white coats and spiraling horns, embodying purity and magic. Graceful and elusive faeries would flutter about, their iridescent wings shimmering with enchantment. Glimpses of phoenixes, with their fiery plumage and rebirth from ashes, would fill her visions with hope and transformation.

Emily's encounters with these ethereal beings were not merely random or fleeting; they held deeper significance. Dragons, unicorns, faeries, and other mystical creatures represented the interconnectedness between the natural and supernatural realms. They symbolized the vast possibilities and hidden wonders that existed beyond the boundaries of ordinary human perception.

These visionary experiences served as sources of inspiration, guiding Emily's understanding of the spiritual forces that shaped the world. They fueled her quest for knowledge and enlightenment, pushing her to explore the depths of her own magical abilities and the mysteries of the universe.

In turn, Emily used her experiences with these mystical creatures to deepen her connection with the natural world. She developed rituals and practices that honored and respected the spirits of these creatures, forging a symbiotic relationship between the magical realm and the earthly plane.

Emily's encounters with dragons and other mystical animals during her trance states were profound and transformative. They expanded her consciousness, revealing the vastness of the supernatural realm and inspiring her to harness her own magical potential. These experiences further reinforced her belief in the intricate web of existence and the intricate beauty that lay hidden within it

In her extraordinary experiences, Emily's connection to the spirit realm extended beyond mystical creatures. During her trance states and heightened spiritual awareness, she would encounter the spirits of deceased kings and queens.

These ethereal encounters brought her face-to-face with the souls of historical figures who had once held great power and influence in their earthly lives. Emily would witness their regal presence, adorned in resplendent attire befitting their status, and surrounded by an aura of authority.

The spirits of the deceased monarchs conveyed a wealth of knowledge, wisdom, and experiences accumulated over their lifetimes. They became sources of inspiration and guidance for Emily, offering insights into leadership, diplomacy, and the intricate tapestry of human history.

Through these encounters, Emily gained a deep appreciation for the legacies left behind by these royal figures. She learned from their triumphs and mistakes, drawing upon their wisdom to inform her own understanding of power, responsibility, and the pursuit of a just and harmonious society.

In turn, the spirits of the kings and queens recognized Emily's unique gifts and her dedication to serving both the living and the dead. They acknowledged her as a bridge between worlds, someone who could carry their messages and honor their memory in the mortal realm.

Emily's encounters with the spirits of deceased monarchs shaped her perspective on the interconnectedness of time and the enduring impact of historical figures. It further deepened her understanding of the spiritual realm and solidified her commitment to using her abilities for the betterment of humanity and the preservation of ancestral wisdom.

These interactions with dead kings and queens served as profound reminders of the vastness of the spirit realm and the collective knowledge that transcends mortal existence. They became integral to Emily's journey, enriching her understanding of both the supernatural and human realms, and inspiring her to fulfill her unique role as a conduit between the living and the departed.

Emily's connection to the spirit realm grew stronger, she found herself engaging in conversations with not only the deceased kings and queens but also with knights and other members of the royal court.

During her trance states or through deliberate meditation, Emily would enter into a state of heightened perception that allowed her to commune with the spirits of these historical figures. She would find herself transported to ancient courts and battlegrounds, where she could interact with the chivalrous knights and the noble royals of the past.

Through these conversations, Emily gained firsthand insights into the codes of honor, loyalty, and bravery that guided the knights. She learned about their quests, their triumphs, and their struggles. Their stories became a source of inspiration, teaching her the importance of integrity, courage, and standing up for what is right.

The conversations with members of the royal court provided a glimpse into the intricacies of governance, diplomacy, and the burdens of leadership. Emily would engage in discussions about political strategies, the challenges of ruling, and the responsibilities that come with power. These encounters offered her valuable lessons on the complexities of societal dynamics and the delicate balance required to maintain a just and prosperous realm.

These dialogues were not one-sided lectures but genuine exchanges of knowledge and ideas. Emily's ability to see and communicate with the spirits of knights and royals allowed her to ask questions, seek guidance, and gain insights that she could apply to her own life and the challenges she faced.

In turn, the spirits of knights and royals recognized the sincerity and curiosity within Emily. They appreciated her desire to learn from their experiences and were eager to share their wisdom with her.

These conversations became an exchange of knowledge and perspectives, fostering a mutual understanding between the living and the departed.

The interactions with knights and royals influenced Emily's journey as a witch and a seeker of wisdom. Their stories and guidance deepened her understanding of honor, leadership, and the complexities of human existence. Their lessons were etched into her consciousness, shaping her character and influencing her actions as she navigated the realms of magic, spirituality, and the human experience.

Emily's conversations with knights and royals served as windows into history and a means of connecting with the collective wisdom of the past. They enriched her understanding of the world, broadened her perspectives, and strengthened her resolve to use her gifts for the betterment of both the living and the departed.

In her encounters and conversations with the spirits of the departed, Emily discovered a profound truth: that in some way, dead people still live. While they may no longer exist in the physical realm, their essence, memories, and consciousness endure in the spiritual realm.

Through her unique ability to communicate with the deceased, Emily experienced firsthand the continued presence and vitality of the spirits. She witnessed their personalities, emotions, and individuality that persisted beyond death. These encounters shattered the conventional notion of death as the complete end of existence, revealing a profound continuity of life in the spiritual realm.

Emily learned that the departed souls retain their identities and carry their memories, desires, and unfinished business with them. They are not mere specters or echoes of the past, but conscious beings who continue to evolve and seek resolution. The spirits of the dead have stories to tell, lessons to impart, and connections to forge with the living.

In her interactions with the spirits, Emily discovered that they yearn for connection, closure, and the opportunity to leave a lasting impact on the world they left behind. They seek acknowledgment, understanding, and sometimes forgiveness. Through her ability to see and converse with them, Emily became a conduit for these desires, helping the spirits find solace and closure.

In this way, Emily's experiences reinforced the belief that the spirits of the departed continue to exist in a meaningful and vibrant way. Their presence offers comfort, guidance, and a reminder of the enduring bonds that transcend the boundaries of life and death.

Emily's realization that dead people still live transformed her understanding of the human experience. It deepened her empathy and fostered a sense of interconnectedness between the living and the departed.

She recognized that the impact we have on others and the connections we forge during our time on Earth reverberate beyond our physical existence, leaving an indelible mark on the tapestry of life.

Through her encounters and conversations with the spirits, Emily became a conduit for bridging the gap between the realms of the living and the dead. She helped bring peace and resolution to the departed souls, while also offering solace and understanding to the living who yearned for connection with their loved ones.

In her stories and experiences, Emily embraced the profound truth that dead people still live, in a spiritual sense, and that their presence can continue to shape and inspire our lives long after they have crossed the threshold of mortality.

Emily's connection with the spirit realm and her ability to communicate with the deceased often led her to seek out cemeteries as places of connection and communion. Cemeteries, with their tranquil atmosphere and abundance of spirits, became natural spaces for Emily to engage in conversations with the departed.

Within the hallowed grounds of the cemetery, Emily would navigate rows of tombstones and mausoleums, guided by her intuition and the energies that called out to her. She would seek out the resting places of those who had passed, feeling drawn to particular individuals based on their spiritual presence or the resonance of their energy.

Once she identified a spirit she wished to connect with, Emily would find a quiet spot nearby, creating a sacred space for communication. She would often light candles, burn incense, and engage in meditative practices to heighten her spiritual awareness and open herself to the presence of the deceased.

Through her focused intent and heightened senses, Emily would initiate conversations with the spirits, offering them a respectful and attentive ear. She would listen to their stories, their regrets, and their desires, providing a compassionate and empathetic presence for them to express themselves.

In these cemetery encounters, Emily acted as a bridge between the living and the dead. She offered solace to the departed souls, allowing them to find closure, resolution, or simply a means to share their experiences and be heard. Through these conversations, she helped the spirits find peace, understanding, and sometimes even guidance for their journey in the afterlife.

Conversely, these interactions also enriched Emily's own understanding of the human experience. She gained insights into the varied perspectives, emotions, and challenges faced by individuals in their life and in the realm beyond. The conversations in cemeteries deepened her empathy, expanded her wisdom, and strengthened her connection to the spiritual fabric that binds all beings.

Emily's visits to cemeteries became a sacred practice, an act of honoring the departed and acknowledging the continuity of life beyond death. She regarded these spaces as places of connection, reflection, and healing, where she could foster a profound exchange of energy and knowledge with the spirits that resided there.

Through her conversations with the dead in cemeteries, Emily not only provided solace and closure to the departed but also cultivated a profound connection to the spiritual realm, deepening her understanding of the human experience and the interconnectedness of all souls, both living and deceased

Emily engages in conversations with the spirits in cemeteries, she would often incorporate chanting songs in various languages into her practices. These melodic incantations served as a means of enhancing her spiritual connection and creating a harmonious atmosphere for communication with the deceased.

Emily had a deep appreciation for the power of sound and its ability to transcend language barriers. Through her studies and exploration of different cultures and mystical traditions, she had acquired a repertoire of chants and songs from various traditions and languages.

The choice of language for her chants depended on the energy she sought to invoke or the specific spirit she wished to connect with. It could range from ancient languages like Latin or Sanskrit to indigenous languages and even her own improvised melodies. Each language carried its own unique vibrations and resonance, allowing Emily to tap into different aspects of the spiritual realm and facilitate communication on a deeper level.

These chants were not merely random sounds but carried intention and meaning. They contained sacred words, invocations, or affirmations that held significance in the spiritual and mystical practices she embraced. The rhythmic repetition of these chants helped Emily enter into a focused and trance- like state, elevating her consciousness and attuning her senses to the spiritual energies surrounding her.

The songs she chanted acted as a bridge between the earthly and the ethereal, drawing the spirits closer and creating a shared vibrational space. They served as a form of communication and invitation, allowing the spirits to recognize her presence and willingly engage in the dialogue.

Furthermore, the melodic and rhythmic nature of the chants had a soothing effect, creating an atmosphere of tranquility and receptivity in the cemetery. It helped both Emily and the spirits find a state of resonance and alignment, facilitating clearer and deeper communication.

The use of different languages in her chants reflected Emily's appreciation for the diverse tapestry of human spirituality and her desire to connect with a broader spectrum of spiritual energies. It exemplified her openness to different cultural traditions and her recognition of the universality of spiritual experiences.

Through her multilingual chants, Emily created a sacred space in the cemeteries, harmonizing the energies of the living and the deceased. It was a practice of honoring the spirit of the place, connecting with the wisdom of different cultures, and fostering a deep sense of unity and understanding between herself and the spirits that resided there.

One fateful day, as Emily ventured into the cemetery with the intention of communing with the spirits, she noticed something peculiar: her supernatural powers had inexplicably vanished. The ability to see and communicate with the dead, the power to move objects, and even her connection to the mystical realm had suddenly abandoned her.

Confusion and disbelief gripped Emily as she tried to comprehend this sudden loss. She searched her mind for answers, trying to recall any events or circumstances that could have triggered such a significant change. But there seemed to be no discernible cause or explanation for the disappearance o her powers.

Fear and uncertainty clouded Emily's thoughts. Her gifts had been an integral part of her identity, and now she felt adrift, cut off from the realm she had come to know and understand. Doubt crept into her heart, and she questioned her purpose and her role as a helper of both the living and the dead.

Despite the loss of her powers, Emily refused to give in to despair. She was determined to find a way t regain what she had lost. She embarked on a journey of self-discovery and exploration, seeking guidance from other practitioners of magic, delving into ancient texts, and consulting with spiritual mentors.

As she ventured into the unknown, Emily discovered that her powers were not permanently extinguished but merely dormant. The sudden loss had served as a catalyst for her growth and transformation. It was a test of her resilience, her dedication, and her willingness to evolve beyond her previous limitations.

During this period of self-reflection and introspection, Emily uncovered new aspects of herself. She realized that her powers were not solely defined by her ability to see dead people and manipulate objects. She possessed innate strengths of empathy, intuition, and compassion that were not contingent on supernatural abilities.

With time, Emily learned to embrace the depth of her inner power and to find solace in the simplicity of her humanity. She discovered that her true gift lay in her capacity to connect with others, to offer support and understanding, and to create positive change in the world through her actions.

While she no longer possessed the same supernatural abilities she once had, Emily's journey through the loss of her powers taught her invaluable lessons about resilience, adaptability, and the essence of true magic. She recognized that true power lies not solely in the external manifestations of supernatura gifts but in the strength of the human spirit and the capacity to make a difference in the lives of others.

Emily's newfound perspective enabled her to continue her path of helping and healing, even without her previous supernatural abilities. She became a source of inspiration for others, sharing her story of resilience and transformation. And in this shared journey of growth and self-discovery, Emily discovered that her powers were never truly lost but had transformed into something even more profound and impactful—her ability to embrace her own humanity and to touch the lives of others wit love and compassion.

As Emily navigated through the uncertainties of her journey and embraced her humanity, a powerful being suddenly materialized before her. Radiating an aura of wisdom and divine presence, this being conveyed a profound message to Emily: she had fulfilled her mission.

The being explained that Emily's path had served a specific purpose, and her journey had been instrumental in bringing about transformation and growth, both within herself and in the lives of those she had touched. Through her interactions with the supernatural, her acts of kindness, and her unwavering dedication to helping others, Emily had accomplished what she was meant to do.

In their conversation, the powerful being unveiled to Emily the ripple effects of her actions—the lives she had influenced, the healing she had facilitated, and the positive changes she had catalyzed. The being emphasized that her mission had never solely been about her supernatural powers but about the impact she had made on the world around her.

With this realization, a sense of fulfillment washed over Emily. She understood that her purpose extended beyond the boundaries of her supernatural abilities. She had touched lives, brought solace to the grieving, and offered hope to those in need. Her mission had been one of compassion, connection, and inspiring others to embrace their own inherent power.

In acknowledging the completion of her mission, the powerful being bestowed upon Emily a gift—a deep sense of inner peace and contentment. The being assured her that her journey would continue, albeit in a different form. Emily would now embark on a new chapter, exploring different avenues of growth, wisdom, and service.

Empowered by this encounter, Emily embraced her newfound understanding of her mission's completion. She recognized that her journey was never meant to be static, but rather a series of transformative chapters that would shape her into the person she was meant to become.

With renewed purpose and gratitude, Emily bid farewell to the powerful being, ready to embark on the next phase of her life's journey. She carried within her heart the lessons learned, the connections made, and the profound impact she had created. And as she ventured forth, she remained open to new possibilities, knowing that her mission had only just begun to unfold in different and unexpected ways.

Inspired by her experiences and the deep connections she had forged with both the living and the departed, Emily made a decision to embark on a new path as a physician specializing in the field of psychology. She recognized that her innate abilities to empathize, listen, and offer support could be channeled into a profession that would allow her to continue helping others on a profound level.

Emily dedicated herself to years of rigorous study and training, immersing herself in the intricacies of the human mind, behavior, and emotional well-being. She sought to understand the complexities of the human psyche and how it intersected with spirituality, grief, and healing.

Armed with her unique perspective and experiences, Emily brought a fresh and compassionate approach to her practice. She offered a safe and nonjudgmental space for her patients, encouraging them to explore their inner worlds, confront their fears, and find the strength to overcome their challenges.

Her background in communicating with spirits and her understanding of the spiritual dimensions of human existence provided a unique lens through which she approached therapy. She integrated concepts of connection, resilience, and the power of the human spirit into her treatment plans, seeking to empower her patients to discover their own inner resources and find meaning in their lives.

Drawing from her encounters with the departed, Emily understood the profound impact of loss, grief, and the longing for connection. She became a guide for those who were grappling with the pain of losing loved ones, offering solace and helping them navigate the intricate journey of healing and acceptance.

Through her work as a physician in the field of psychology, Emily continued to touch lives, instilling hope, and facilitating transformative change. Her unique background and experiences lent depth and richness to her therapeutic approach, making her a trusted and revered figure in the field.

Emily's story became an inspiration to her patients and colleagues alike. She demonstrated that healing and personal growth can emerge from the most unexpected sources, and that one's life experiences, even those involving the supernatural, can shape and enhance their professional journey.

As she delved deeper into her career, Emily remained open to the mysterious and unseen aspects of life. She understood that there was much that science and psychology couldn't explain, and she embraced the interconnectedness of mind, body, and spirit in her practice.

Through her dedication, compassion, and unique blend of psychological expertise and spiritual insights, Emily continued to make a profound difference in the lives of those she served. Her journey as a physician in the field of psychology became a testament to the enduring power of empathy, the significance of personal growth, and the transformative nature of embracing one's calling.

After completing her studies and gaining valuable experience in the field of psychology, Emily felt a calling to establish her own practice in a serene and close-knit community. She discovered the perfect setting in a small town called Whiteflies—a place known for its picturesque landscapes, warm-hearted residents, and a deep appreciation for holistic well-being.

With a vision to provide comprehensive mental health care that embraced both traditional psychological approaches and her unique insights gained from her supernatural experiences, Emily opened the doors to her practice in Whiteflies. She created a nurturing and welcoming space, where individuals seeking support and healing could find solace and guidance.

Word quickly spread throughout the town about Emily's empathetic nature, her holistic approach, and her remarkable ability to connect with her patients on a profound level. The community embraced her with open arms, recognizing her genuine desire to make a difference in their lives.

In her practice, Emily offered a wide range of services to cater to the diverse needs of the town's residents. She provided individual therapy sessions, group counseling, workshops on self-care and personal growth, and even incorporated alternative therapies such as meditation, mindfulness, and expressive arts into her practice.

The townspeople of Whiteflies found solace in Emily's compassionate and nonjudgmental approach. They felt seen, heard, and understood as she worked alongside them, unraveling their emotional complexities and guiding them towards healing and self-discovery.

Through her practice, Emily cultivated a deep sense of community. She facilitated support groups where individuals could connect with others who had experienced similar challenges. She organized community events focused on mental health awareness, inviting guest speakers and experts to share their knowledge and insights.

Emily's reputation extended beyond Whiteflies, drawing people from neighboring towns who sought her guidance and expertise. Her practice became a beacon of hope, a place where individuals could find refuge from the storms of their minds and hearts, knowing they would be met with compassion and understanding.

In her small town practice, Emily found fulfillment beyond measure. She witnessed the transformative power of therapy, witnessing her patients regain their strength, find resilience, and reclaim their lives. She celebrated their victories, big and small, as they stepped into their authentic selves and embraced a renewed sense of purpose and joy.

As the years passed, Emily's practice flourished, and the impact of her work radiated throughout the community. She became an integral part of Whiteflies, weaving her compassionate presence into the fabric of the town's collective well-being.

Emily's story became intertwined with the stories of the townspeople she served. Her journey from a young woman with supernatural gifts to a renowned psychologist in Whiteflies showcased the transformative power of embracing one's unique abilities, following one's calling, and creating a space for healing and growth.

And in the quiet tranquility of Whiteflies, Emily found her purpose—a purpose that transcended her supernatural origins and allowed her to make a profound and lasting impact on the lives of others

As Emily's powers surged back into her life, she soon realized that they came with a heavy price. Unbeknownst to her, the raw, untamed magic coursing through her veins began to take a toll on her physical form.

At first, subtle changes appeared—a few wrinkles etched across her face, strands of gray weaving through her hair. But as time went on, the transformation accelerated, leaving Emily with a visage that betrayed her youthful appearance. Her once vibrant and radiant countenance gave way to a withered and weathered facade.

Her teeth, once strong and pearly white, began to decay and fall out, leaving gaps in her smile. Her nails grew long and twisted, resembling talons that seemed to reflect the untamed nature of her powers. Emily was left to grapple with a body that no longer aligned with her vibrant spirit.

The townspeople of Whiteflies, who had come to trust and admire Emily, were taken aback by her physical transformation. Whispers filled the air, questioning the source of her powers and the toll they had exacted upon her. Some grew fearful, associating her appearance with dark magic and malevolence.

But amid the external changes, Emily's spirit remained resilient. She refused to allow her physical appearance to define her or dampen her determination to use her powers for good. Though her body now reflected the weight of her magic, she saw it as a reminder of the sacrifices she had willingly embraced in her quest to help others.

Emily sought solace in her connection with the supernatural realm. Through meditation and introspection, she discovered that her physical changes were not solely a consequence of her powers but also a symbol of her deep connection to the mystical forces that flowed through her.

With the support of trusted allies and her unwavering inner strength, Emily learned to harness and channel her magic in a more controlled manner. She sought guidance from wise beings who

understood the delicate balance between power and physicality, aiding her in finding harmony within herself.

While her physical appearance remained altered, Emily's newfound control over her powers allowed her to continue her work in Whiteflies. She persisted in offering her healing services, touching the lives of those in need, and helping them navigate their own struggles with compassion and understanding.

As time went on, the townspeople began to see past Emily's external changes and appreciate the wisdom, empathy, and unwavering dedication that radiated from her. They recognized that her transformation was a testament to her unwavering commitment to the greater good, even at great personal cost.

Emily's physical appearance, marked by the toll of her powers, became a symbol of her unwavering resilience and her commitment to serving others. The townspeople, once apprehensive, came to see her as a beacon of strength and inspiration—a living reminder of the sacrifices one can make in the pursuit of helping others.

Despite her physical transformation, Emily's impact on the lives of the townspeople remained profound. Her presence continued to be sought after and cherished, as she provided guidance, healing, and a source of hope for those in need.

Her journey became a testament to the enduring power of inner strength and the ability to overcome adversity. Through her selflessness, Emily taught the people of Whiteflies that true beauty lies not in outward appearances, but in the depth of one's character and the compassion that emanates from within.

And as Emily carried on with her mission, embracing her altered physical form as a badge of honor, she became a revered figure in the town—a living testament to the resilience of the human spirit and the transformative power of embracing one's calling, no matter the challenges that come along the way.

As Emily fully embraced her identity as a witch, the people of Whiteflies continued to embrace her with love and admiration, seeing beyond the external changes that her powers had wrought. They ecognized the depth of her compassion, her unwavering dedication to their well-being, and the positive impact she had on their lives.

With her newfound mastery over her magic, Emily honed her skills and expanded her repertoire of abilities. She learned to harness the power of flight, gracefully soaring through the night sky astride a broomstick, a symbol of her connection to the ancient traditions of witchcraft. The townspeople marveled at her enchanting displays, viewing her flights not as a display of otherworldly power, but as a testament to her courage, freedom, and connection to the mystical realms.

In Whiteflies, the sight of Emily gliding through the air on her broomstick became a source of wonder and inspiration. Children gazed up at her with wide-eyed excitement, dreaming of the possibilities that lay beyond the limitations of the mundane world. The townspeople embraced the enchantment that she brought to their lives, seeing it as a reminder of the magic that exists within each of them.

Emily's flights on her broomstick also served a practical purpose. She would journey to distant places, seeking out rare herbs and mystical artifacts to enhance her healing practices. With each flight, she expanded her knowledge and brought back treasures that enriched the lives of those she served.

Her ability to fly allowed her to connect with nature in profound ways. She would soar high above the treetops, communing with the spirits of the land and seeking their guidance. She developed a deep understanding of the natural world and the interconnectedness of all living beings, incorporating this wisdom into her therapeutic approaches.

The people of Whiteflies reveled in Emily's magical presence, often seeking her counsel for matters both mundane and extraordinary. She became a trusted confidante, offering guidance, spells, and rituals to address a variety of challenges and desires. Whether it was love, protection, abundance, or personal growth, Emily's wisdom and magical prowess were sought after by many.

Despite her increasingly powerful magical abilities, Emily remained grounded and committed to her role as a healer. She continued to run her practice, providing psychological support, counseling, and therapeutic interventions. Her magical and psychological expertise complemented each other, allowing her to offer a holistic approach to healing that touched the hearts and souls of her patients.

In the eyes of the townspeople, Emily's transformation into a full-blooded witch was not a cause for fear or rejection. Rather, it served as a testament to the resilience of the human spirit and the acceptance of the extraordinary in their everyday lives. They embraced her as an integral part of their community, recognizing her as a force of light, wisdom, and profound compassion.

Emily's story became a cherished legend in Whiteflies, passed down through generations, inspiring individuals to embrace their unique gifts, pursue their passions, and stand tall in the face of adversity. She became a symbol of courage, authenticity, and the limitless possibilities that exist when one dares to embrace their true nature.

And as Emily continued to fly on her broomstick, her heart filled with gratitude for the love and acceptance she received from the people of Whiteflies. Together, they forged a bond that transcended the boundaries of the ordinary, weaving a tapestry of magic, compassion, and community that would endure for generations to come

As Emily's reputation as a compassionate and powerful witch grew, the people of Whiteflies bestowed upon her a new name: Emeli the Good Witch. This name reflected the deep respect and love they held for her, symbolizing her unwavering commitment to using her powers for the betterment of others.

The townspeople came to recognize Emeli as a beacon of hope, a source of wisdom, and a guiding light in their lives. They sought her out not only for her magical abilities but also for her empathetic nature and her ability to understand the complexities of the human experience.

Emeli's presence in Whiteflies became synonymous with healing, both of the body and the soul. People from far and wide sought her assistance, traveling great distances to experience her transformative touch. From the youngest child to the oldest elder, all found solace and comfort in her compassionate care.

Her practice thrived as word of her remarkable abilities spread. She employed her knowledge of psychology, her deep connection to the mystical realms, and her innate intuition to provide holistic healing to those who sought her aid. Her therapeutic interventions were enhanced by her magical spells, rituals, and potions, ensuring a comprehensive approach to well-being.

Emeli's impact extended beyond the boundaries of her practice. She took an active role in community affairs, using her influence and magical prowess to bring harmony, abundance, and protection to the town. She organized festivals, where the townspeople would come together to celebrate the seasons, honor the spirits, and embrace the enchantment that surrounded them.

The title of "Emeli the Good Witch" was not just a name; it was a testament to her character and the profound effect she had on the lives of others. The people of Whiteflies recognized her as a force of light in a sometimes dark world, a bridge between the ordinary and the extraordinary.

Emeli, in turn, approached her newfound title with humility and grace. She understood the weight of the responsibility that came with being seen as a paragon of goodness. She continued to deepen her knowledge, refine her magical abilities, and expand her understanding of the human psyche. With each passing day, she strove to become an even better version of herself, a beacon of inspiration to others.

Her connection to the supernatural realms remained strong. Dragons, spirits, and mythical creatures continued to visit her in dreams and visions, offering guidance and insight into the mysteries of the universe. Emeli cherished these encounters, using the wisdom she gained to further her own growth and share it with those she encountered.

In the eyes of the townspeople, Emeli was not just a witch, but a guardian of their collective well-being. They trusted her implicitly, seeking her counsel during times of uncertainty, celebrating with her in times of joy, and finding solace in her presence during times of sorrow.

Emeli's story became intertwined with the history and folklore of Whiteflies. Her name would be passed down through the generations, spoken with reverence and gratitude. Even long after her time on

Earth had passed, the memory of Emeli the Good Witch would endure as a symbol of love, compassion, and the profound impact one individual can have on an entire community.

And so, Emeli continued her journey, walking the delicate path between magic and humanity, spreading light and healing wherever she went. Her legacy lived on, not just in the tales told of her extraordinary abilities, but in the hearts of those whose lives she touched. The name "Emeli the Good Witch" echoed through the ages, a testament to the transformative power of compassion, courage, and the pursuit of goodness in a world that sometimes yearns for magic.

Every evening at 6 PM, as the sun began to dip below the horizon, the children of Whiteflies would gather on the grassy field, eagerly awaiting the arrival of Emeli the Good Witch on her broomstick. Their eyes sparkled with excitement, their imaginations soaring as they anticipated the magical sight that was about to unfold.

As the clock struck six, a hush fell over the crowd, and a gentle breeze seemed to carry the whispers of anticipation through the air. And there she was, Emeli, gracefully soaring through the sky on her

broomstick. The children cheered and clapped, their laughter blending with the joyous sound of the wind rustling through the trees.

Emeli would perform intricate aerial maneuvers, twirling and spinning with an effortless grace. She would dip low, nearly brushing the tips of the grass, before soaring back up into the sky, leaving trails of stardust in her wake. Her broomstick seemed an extension of herself, as if it danced with her in perfect harmony.

The children would watch in awe, their gazes locked on Emeli as she weaved her way through the evening sky. They marveled at her ethereal presence, feeling a sense of wonder and possibility fill their young hearts. Some would even try to mimic her movements, their outstretched arms pretending to guide their own imaginary broomsticks.

Emeli's flights on her broomstick became a cherished ritual, a time of enchantment and pure delight for the children of Whiteflies. They would wave and call out to her, their voices filled with adoration and admiration. Emeli would respond with a warm smile and a playful wink, creating a sense of connection that touched their souls.

For those brief moments, the boundaries between reality and magic blurred. The children believed in the extraordinary, embracing the notion that anything was possible. Emeli's flights inspired their dreams, encouraging them to nurture their own unique gifts and find the magic within themselves.

As the sky darkened and the stars emerged, Emeli would bid the children farewell, promising to return on another evening. The children would wave goodbye, their faces illuminated by the twinkle in their eyes. They carried the memory of Emeli's flights in their hearts, knowing that the world held secrets and wonders beyond their wildest imagination.

And so, the tradition continued, with each passing day bringing new children to the grassy field, eagerly awaiting the magical spectacle that unfolded at 6 PM. Emeli, the Good Witch, delighted in the joy she brought to their lives, cherishing the connection she shared with the younger generation.

Her evening flights on her broomstick became a symbol of hope, wonder, and the enduring power of imagination. The children of Whiteflies grew up with tales of Emeli's flights, passing down the stories from one generation to the next. They would reminisce about their own experiences, sharing the enchantment with their own children, keeping the magic alive.

Emeli, with her broomstick as her loyal companion, continued to grace the evening skies of Whiteflies, reminding both young and old that magic can be found in the simplest of moments. Her flights were not just a spectacle; they were a testament to the enduring belief that wonder and enchantment exist all around us if we are open to seeing them.

And so, as the sun set on another day, the children of Whiteflies would gather on the grass, their eyes fixed on the horizon, eagerly awaiting the arrival of Emeli the Good Witch on her broomstick. And with each flight, their hearts would soar alongside her, forever touched by the magic that danced through their lives.

Emily, the Good Witch, was always dressed in a flowing white gown as she graced the skies of Whiteflies on her broomstick. Her ethereal presence was accentuated by the pristine white fabric that billowed around her, symbolizing purity, light, and the goodness that radiated from within her.

As she soared through the evening sky, the children of Whiteflies would marvel at the sight of Emily's white-clad figure, contrasting against the backdrop of the darkening sky. To them, the choice of white represented her benevolent nature, her unwavering dedication to helping others, and her connection to the forces of light and goodness.

The children, and indeed the entire community, held Emily close to their hearts as she disappeared into the distance, leaving behind an indelible mark on their lives. They would reminisce about her magical flights, her wise counsel, and the profound impact she had on their town. Her memory would forever be etched in their collective consciousness, a symbol of hope, love, and the power of embracing one's true self.

Even though Emily never returned physically, her legacy lived on. Her story, filled with enchantment and compassion, would be passed down from generation to generation, ensuring that her presence and the lessons she taught would endure. The people of Whiteflies would forever hold her dear, cherishing the memories and the inspiration she left behind.

And so, Emily, the Good Witch, remained eternally present in the hearts of the people she touched. Her departure into the distance only heightened the sense of wonder and mystery surrounding her. Though she may have vanished from their sight, her spirit and her influence continued to weave through the fabric of their lives, forever reminding them of the magic that resides within each of them.

As the years passed, the people of Whiteflies would recall their encounters with Emily with fondness and gratitude. They would look up at the evening sky, where she once soared, and feel a sense of connection to something greater than themselves. They would carry her teachings of love, compassion, and embracing one's true nature throughout their lives, ensuring that her legacy would endure for generations to come.

And so, as the twilight settled over Whiteflies, the town would forever hold Emily in their hearts. They would remember her white-clad figure gliding through the skies, bringing joy, wonder, and a touch of

magic to their lives. Her story would continue to be told, inspiring new generations to believe in the extraordinary and to embrace the power of goodness and love.

In the hearts and minds of the people of Whiteflies, Emily would forever be a symbol of light, a guardian of dreams, and a reminder that the magic we seek resides within us all. Her memory would forever be cherished, her name spoken with reverence and gratitude, and her legacy carried on the wings of imagination and wonder.

I extend my heartfelt gratitude for embarking on this literary journey with me. Your presence and engagement have been the driving force behind the words that have come to life on these pages. Each line, every story, and the shared moments of creativity have been enriched by your time and attention.

Whether you've delved into tales of whimsy, explored the depths of emotions, or simply sought a moment of escape, your readership has been the cornerstone of this literary adventure. Your curiosity, feedback, and appreciation have inspired me to weave narratives that resonate and linger in the tapestry of imagination.

In the realm of words, readers are the true alchemists, transforming mere text into living, breathing stories. Your interpretations, reflections, and connections with the written word breathe life into the narratives crafted here. It is your minds that give wings to the stories, allowing them to soar beyond the confines of the page.

Thank you for being the companions on this literary odyssey. Your presence has turned the solitary act of writing into a shared experience, and for that, I am profoundly grateful. May our journey through words continue, and may each story find its echo in the chambers of your hearts.

With sincere appreciation,

Credit: Google. Safari, Internet explorer, open ai, and all web search engines.

*Angel Viera, Author*

( CR 2023) THE END